The Political Theater of
Early Seventeenth-Century Spain,
with Special Reference to
Juan Ruiz de Alarcón

Ibérica

A. Robert Lauer
General Editor

Vol. 6

PETER LANG
New York • San Francisco • Bern • Baltimore
Frankfurt am Main • Berlin • Wien • Paris

Cynthia Leone Halpern

The Political Theater of Early Seventeenth-Century Spain, with Special Reference to Juan Ruiz de Alarcón

To Holy Spirit Library of Cabrini College

Cynthia Leone Halpern
2-15-95

PETER LANG
New York • San Francisco • Bern • Baltimore
Frankfurt am Main • Berlin • Wien • Paris

Library of Congress Cataloging-in-Publication Data

Halpern, Cynthia Leone.
   The political theater of early seventeenth-century Spain,
with special reference to Juan Ruiz de Alarcón / by Cynthia
Leone Halpern.
      p. cm. — (Ibérica ; v. 6)
   Includes bibliographical references and index.
   1. Spanish drama—Classical period, 1500-1700—History
and criticism.   2. Political plays, Spanish—History and
criticism.   3. Ruiz de Alarcón, Juan, 1580?-1639—Political
and social views.   I. Title.   II. Series: Ibérica (New York,
N.Y.) ; vol. 6.
PQ6109.H35   1993   862'.309358—dc20   92-20890
ISBN 0-8204-1976-1   CIP
ISSN 1056-5000

Die Deutsche Bibliothek-CIP-Einheitsaufnahme

Leone Halpern, Cynthia:
The political theater of early seventeenth-century Spain with
special reference to Juan Ruiz de Alarcón / Cynthia Leone
Halpern.—New York; Bern; Berlin; Frankfurt/M.; Paris; Wien:
Lang, 1993
      (Ibérica ; Vol. 6)
      ISBN 0-8204-1976-1
   NE: GT

Cover Design by George Lallas.

The paper in this book meets the guidelines for permanence
and durability of the Committee on Production Guidelines
for Book Longevity of the Council on Library Resources.

© Peter Lang Publishing, Inc., New York 1993

Printed in the United States of America.

DEDICATION

To my teacher, Willard F. King, with gratitude.

TABLE OF CONTENTS

PREFACE

The primary intention of this study is to examine the dramas of Juan Ruiz de Alarcón (1581?–1639) which deal with political themes. This dramatist lived during the critical period of the Spanish monarchies of both Philip III and Philip IV when the fortunes of the State were rapidly declining, and the powerful empire of Charles V and Philip II showed signs of decay. Concerned by these alarming developments, Alarcón wrote a number of plays dealing with the nature of kingship, the relation between the king and his first minister the *privado* (also known as the *valido*), the need for reform of the state, and the relation of the king to the law. It is a theater which comments on the political problems of his day, even though the plays are ostensibly set in medieval Spain or ancient Greece. The playwright is not concerned about the historical accuracy of his plays, preferring to "skirt the complexities of the historical world in favor of some 'higher' and less time-bound mode of thinking and feeling."[1] Moral truth, good for all times, was his aim, not the faithful recreation of past historical epochs.[2] This dramatist was much perturbed by the faltering morality of his day and by increasing political corruption. Alarcón was far from alone in feeling and responding to the need for reform, but he devoted a larger proportion of his theater to the dramatization of political problems than did any other major playwright of the times. Perhaps his lengthy training as a lawyer explains his special sensitivity to problems of law and the role of the monarch in maintaining a healthy body politic.

To entertain his audiences Alarcón used the typical devices of the Lopean comedia, i.e., lively dialogues, complicated love intrigues, the whimsical character of the *gracioso*, duels and rapes, as well as the occasional well-made sonnet. But the message of his political dramas must not be obscured by these trappings. He was simply a master practitioner of the Horatian doctrine of *utile dulce* (or, as so often repeated in the seventeenth century, *deleitar enseñando*). Every play studied here, as the reader of this essay will observe, makes use of these devices. Unfortunately, today's readers or viewers of Alarcón's political theater, removed as they are from the crucial problems of Alarcón's society, seldom perceive the serious message behind the surface excitement. Or, at the most, the contemporary reader may discern a conflict between, let us say, free will and predestination, as is so often seen in discussions of *El dueño de las estrellas,* which really focuses on the ultimate sacrifice a *privado* may be compelled to make in order to maintain his loyalty to the absolute monarch. For this reason, I devote this study to the elucidation of the *utile* aspect of the dramas considered, i.e., political commentary.

Alarcón's thought may not be particularly original, but he was obviously well read in the political and reform literature of his day, as the reader of his plays today all too often is not. If we are to understand and appreciate this important segment of his theater, it behooves us then to consider first the most influential political theorists of the time as well as the major problems facing Spanish society in the early seventeenth century. Thus, the first part of this study deals with a) theories of kingship and law, b) the rise and importance of the king's *privado*, c) the political, social and economic problems of the period.

Next, in order to deepen the perspective on Alarcón's work, attention is given to political plays by three contemporaries of Alarcón, the immensely popular Lope de Vega, the Mercedarian friar Tirso de Molina and the satirist Francisco de Quevedo. Troubled and critical as these writers sometimes were about problems of government, their political plays do not deal as systematically or as completely as do Alarcón's dramas with the relations between the king, his ministers, and the health of the state and its people. Chapters V and VI of this study treat in detail the seven major political plays of Juan Ruiz de Alarcón.

NOTES

[1] Herbert Lindenberger, *Historical Drama—The Relation of Literature and Reality* (Chicago and London: The U of Chicago P, 1975), p. 115.

[2] Lindenberger, p. 110.

CHAPTER I
INFLUENTIAL THEORIES OF KINGSHIP

The following discussion focuses on two late sixteenth-century theorists—out of the many political theorists of this time—because they represent the extreme poles of argument about the theory of monarchy. Jean Bodin is the spokesman for absolutism with few or no checks. Juan de Mariana went as far as possible in his day in suggesting limitations on sovereign power.

A. Jean Bodin

Clearly among the most influential of contemporary political theorists was the Frenchman Jean Bodin (1530?–1596), who believed that an absolutist, divinely ordained political authority was the ideal form of government. He studied law at the University of Toulouse and after graduation continued residence there to lecture on Roman law. A humanist and an advocate of educational reform, he is most celebrated for his ideas on sovereignty. His best-known work is *La République* (1577, translated into Spanish in 1590 under the title *Los seis libros de la República* and into English in 1606 called *The Six Bookes of a Commonweale*), in which he attempts to define the state in a very distinct way. He insists that the state must have one supreme political authority. Authority for Bodin was the foundation of his entire system of politics. He stresses that the most fundamental of the various rights of the Crown was the power to make laws, that is, as the chief legislator of the state.[1] In medieval thought the functions of the ruler that were emphasized were the judicial and administrative duties. The sixteenth and seventeenth centuries, however, saw a great deal of visible and rapid social change, and Bodin realized that it was also necessary for the rulers to be able to meet these changing conditions with new laws.[2]

In the *République*, Bodin emphasizes that sovereignty must be perpetual with an unconditional grant of power for life. He also stresses that sovereignty must be absolute. There can be no individual or group superior in authority to a true monarch. His absolute authority means that the sovereign is not bound even by the laws of his country.[3] His power is unlimited, and he can make new laws or change old ones in whatever way he sees fit.

In Bodin's political system, the sovereign is certainly at the peak of power here on earth, since he considers the sovereign the "lieutenant" of God upon earth.[4] There is, however, an even higher authority found in the laws of God. The sovereign operates in a world governed by divine and natural law.[5] "Like most of his contemporaries, he firmly believed that the sovereign is directly responsible to God, and he had an unquestioning faith in divine retribution for actions which contravened the higher law."[6] In other words, the king, just like his subjects, must also fear God. When it is a question of only earthly power, however, Bodin supports the doctrine of nonresistance to the authority of the king, since the responsibility of a subject is to obey the monarch without ever questioning his command and to leave punishment of a king's misguided actions to God alone. On the other hand, if the monarch chooses to behave in a manner which is contrary to divine or natural order, the subject need not obey. Active resistance or rebellion is, however, precluded.[7]

A "fairly precise meaning" of natural law had already evolved by this time in European jurisprudence. Many definitions of natural law have been attempted for centuries, but the generally accepted notion of natural law has been explained as the ultimate norm of right and wrong, as the paradigm of life according to Nature, as a law which arises from the universal dictates of human nature and which has no necessary connection to the man-made codes established by Church and State. Self-defense, the right to defend against an attack on one's body and life, is a constant for all ages and cultures. "The basic precepts of natural law had been formulated in Roman law..." Bodin, as we know, lectured on Roman law, and as a lawyer, "was thoroughly familiar" with the Roman concept of natural law. He uses natural law as a basis for two of the limitations which he places upon the sovereign.[8] First Bodin believes that a ruler, like his subjects, *should* obey the laws of the country although he is not bound in any way by these laws (see footnote 3). In order to maintain social order, the subjects must feel confident that their king is keeping the faith by assuring that these covenants are preserved. The king, therefore, should set himself up as the ultimate pattern for his subjects. He should show respect to his oath and duty as king by incorporating his laws and contracts into his own life, although, to repeat, he is certainly not bound to do so.[9] Secondly, he urges the inviolability of private property rights, believing that property rights are protected by natural law.[10] He is also of the conviction that since natural law is superior to the sovereign, subjects have the right to consent to taxation. He believes that the implementation of taxation should be carried out by either of the representative bodies, the Estates General or the regional estates, but stresses that neither of these assemblies has any authority apart from the king.[11] Certainly as far as legislation is concerned, the estates are inferior to the monarch. Bodin insists that on earth the king's authority is indivisible and absolute and can be shared with no one.

In the *République* he traces the origin of the state to the family unit.[12] He sees the father as the patriarchal authority of the family and compares his control over the rest of the family with that of the king over his subjects. He regards fatherhood as the only natural source of power and a model to follow in the formation of the ideal commonwealth[13] and explains his theory with an illustration from nature, in which monarchy can be detected in every corner of the universe. It is a fact that every form of animal life follows its natural leader.[14] There is, for example, "the king among the bees, the leader in the herd, the buck among the flocks...gold among the metals, the sun among the stars..."[15]

He also makes the comparison of the human body to that of "the body of the state." It is natural that all parts of the human body obey one head where the brain is constantly functioning. It then must logically follow that the people of the state should obey their one sovereign.[16] The authority of the sovereign over his subjects corresponds to that of God over the universe. It must not be considered servitude for a child to obey his father, but rather a fact of nature. It is equally natural for a citizen to follow the command of his king.[17] Our world is made up of many unequal parts, but harmony in our universe is found through dissimilarity. The best republic would be the one that imitates nature, which is held together by a multitude of discordant elements. Bodin believes that the same is true of a harmonious melody, in that a pleasing harmony is achieved only by the coming together of "dissimilar notes." The state, like nature, must also be a mixture of dissimilarities ranging from the highest level to the lowest level, each man doing his part in the construction of a peaceful existence.[18]

Bodin believes that there can be excellence in numbers only when unity exists.[19] A single ruler is much more capable of reducing conflict in the state. Harmony and order prevail when there is only one controlling force. In *The Six Bookes of a Commonweale,* Bodin explains that just as the world is ruled by only one God, so too should a well-governed state have a single monarch.[20] The presence of too many officials allows for the breeding of avarice, since each one wishes himself to be the ruler and the receiver of riches. On the other hand, with only just a few worthy magistrates, the citizens will feel inspired to imitate their virtue and example.[21]

The ideal monarch in Bodin's eyes is one who understands that he has come into this world for the true worship of God and feels bound by his oath and duty as Prince to rule the state in agreement with the fundamental laws and customs of the state for the public good.[22] The supreme safety of the state and of all the laws depends on this. A monarch should realize that his power is most effective when he adheres to the precepts of religion. He should be "so informed by training that he realizes that God is the judge and spectator of all his actions," and "will do nothing impious or wicked, will not even think of anything base. This one man his subjects will love and fear." They will model their lives and habits by his virtuous example.[23]

The legitimate monarch becomes a tyrant when he puts personal passion above public good and repays faithful ministers with ingratitude.[24] Bodin gives the example of Dionysius the Younger, "whom his father reared in ease and delight so that he was not brought into the public eye from the training field, was not hardened by any discipline at all, and had no appreciation of true merit. So he indulged his many desires in company with the most dangerous flatterers, until he was driven from that tyranny as from a citadel."[25] The monarch who searches for glory must realize that true value consists of virtue alone, and he must, therefore, reject improper behavior. In this way he may "control the wicked, guard the good, and honor the deeds of the brave and the wise with praises and rewards to the everlasting shame of the wicked."[26] The fear of God will ensure that a king serve the interests of the nation well. The aim of a legitimate king must be honor; self-gratification is the aim of the tyrant.

The prince should hold in esteem the laws which he has made for his kingdom.[27] If a king, guided by passion rather than reason, is overcome by the power of his position and begins to transgress the laws which he himself has constituted, it is then the duty of the chief ministers to help direct him back to the correct path. Bodin admitted that a magistrate might "refuse to obey" an unjust command contrary to his oath, but in general he should set himself up as an example of submission. Still a magistrate ought not to obey the commands of his monarch "...if such commands bee contrarie to the lawes of nature."[28]

To repeat Bodin's viewpoint, it is the responsibility of the prince to understand that he has been born into this world for the true worship of God. He must recognize that God is the supreme judge and spectator of all his actions. A sovereign must be nurtured and taught properly the ways befitting a king. He must come to understand that true worth can be measured by acts of virtue alone. A tyrant, on the other hand, totally loses sight of this purpose, desiring, more than the safety of his subjects, the fulfillment of his own passion. Yet if it happens that a true monarch lapses into tyranny, Bodin insists that "...it is not lawfull for any man living, of himselfe to invade the soveraigntie, and to make himselfe maister of his fellowes, what colour of vertue or iustice soeuer they pretend: and that more is, in law he is guiltie of death, that wrongfully taketh vppon him any of the markes proper vnto soueraigne maiestïe."[29] In other words, according to Bodin, it is simply unlawful for the subjects to attempt anything against the honor, life or dignity of their sovereign prince even though he may have committed an act of wickedness, impiety or cruelty.[30] Bodin is careful to warn a sovereign that any tyrannical actions on his part may incite the populace to sedition and lead to the destruction of the state. He insists, however, that it is no one's right to decide on his own that the prince is a tyrant. If every citizen were given such a right, there could be no possible order. The prince must be supreme and his sovereignty wholly absolute.[31]

In sum, Bodin is keenly opposed to those doctrines which would not hesitate to expel princes suspected of tyranny, believing that those theories which advocate the punishment of a tyrannical ruler are to be considered as anarchy. As a loyal subject of the king of France, Bodin repudiates the monarchomachist doctrine which allows the punishment and even death of a misguided sovereign.

In general, Bodin does not believe that consent of the subjects in matters of state is of importance, since the authority of the king is unlimited. Thus parliaments are subordinate to the king in legislation, and the king is not subject to the authority of the estates or the nobles of the kingdom. The function of the estates, in Bodin's firm opinion, was that of providing subjects with an opportunity of simply presenting their humble petitions. It was the king's right, however, to dissolve or convoke the estates in whatever way he saw fit . The sovereign is never to be under the power or will of the estates. The sovereignty of the monarch is never to be considered as diminished by the estates, but increased by their existence, since it is through the estates that his sovereignty is most unequivocally recognized.[32]

Although Bodin does give the parliament the right to plead in protest against a regal order, he is generally opposed to such a right for fear of the acceptance of public disobedience to the monarch. He believes that a magistrate of the king should be an example of obedience for all to follow. Bodin goes so far as to say that conscience and religion should not come into play when a subject is commanded by his king.[33] In the final part of this study, several plays of Alarcón will be discussed which illustrate exactly this principle. Obedience to one's own king is held by Alarcón to be one of the supreme virtues of a Spanish courtier, especially, perhaps, when the latter's personal interests are at stake.

Even though, as we have seen, Bodin places certain limitations on monarchical absolutism (the prince is bound by divine and natural law, and as a monarch it is advisable that he respect his own laws), it is important to note that Bodin does not emphasize these limitations on a sovereign; rather he stresses what the king is capable of doing. The center of his thinking, therefore, is not that the king is limited, but that he is powerful, and since kingship was instituted by God, the king is master in politics, and disobedience to his word is of the gravest consequence. The sovereign, according to Bodin, should be obeyed since his kingly status inherently entitles him to obedience. If the opportunity should arise, however, when the ruler cannot properly exert his power in matters of domestic law, he must then turn to his established councillors for advice.

B. Juan de Mariana

There were, of course, spokesmen for the constitutionalist approach to government, and the lawyer Alarcón also drew inspiration in some degree from them. The leading advocate of this constitutional approach to government was clearly Juan de Mariana (1536–1624), of the Society of Jesus. Like Bodin, Mariana witnessed the rise of Spain to world hegemony, but surviving him by nearly thirty years, he also lived to see Spain's decline under the reign of the weak grandson of Emperor Charles, Philip III. His most important work, the *Historia general de España,* published in Latin (*Historiae de rebus Hispaniae*) in 1592, was published in 1601 in a Spanish translation made by Mariana himself. In 1599, *De rege et regis institutione* (*Del rey y de la institución real*) appeared; and in 1609 his *Tractatus septem* (*Siete tratados*), which includes his treatise *De monetae mutatione* (*Sobre la alteración de la moneda*), dangerously critical of the inflation under Philip III, were published. It is in his work *De rege* that he first set forth his theory of government. Mariana is not an enemy of the monarchical form of government, but he insists that it must be constitutional.[34] He was a follower of the scholastic tradition of Francisco de Vitoria (1483–1546) and other political thinkers such as Francisco Suárez (1548–1617) and Luis de Molina (1535–1601), but with many deviating attitudes. Unlike many earlier political theorists, he developed his political doctrine through history rather than from theology. He spent eight years living in Italy and was much influenced by humanist writing, and like Machiavelli and Guicciardini, he similarly combined history and political theory.[35]

Mariana views government as a distinctly human creation. He sees the state not as a law of nature which is derived from God but formed by man's inherent reason and will and stemming from the innate need of man for other men, which of course is inspired by God.[36] In other words, the state came into existence with the purpose of serving man's earthly wants and needs. He considers man as a creature who is born helpless, yet at the same time gifted with a God-given reason which allows and guides him to provide for his needs. The self-defense of mankind must naturally be found in the companionship of his fellow men.[37] Following the scholastic tradition of Vitoria, Mariana believes that God had created man with a particular constitution and make-up, leaving him the formation of a society as his only source of self-defense.[38] Following the scholastics also, Mariana sees monarchy as a natural formation stemming from the civil society. "The scholastic tradition …always postulated that society could not exist without government, without submission to some superior power."[39] The monarchy was constituted as a result of man's need for government and his consequent readiness to yield some of his rights to a superior power in order to se-

cure the benefits of a stable government. The point which must be
stressed is that Mariana insists that the existence of the monarchy is a result of a definite "human decision" and, therefore, for the sake of the
community's survival and benefit, the monarch must be obeyed.[40]

A striking dissimilarity between Mariana and Bodin can be found in
their views on dealing with a tyrannical ruler. Bodin's wholly absolutist,
divine-right theory sees the monarch as the natural source of power on
earth and not to be questioned since he was given to man by God.
Mariana, on the other hand, boldly challenges the boundless authority of
kings and defends the right of resistance to a tyrant.

Bodin is firm in his insistence that no man has the right to decide if
his prince is a tyrant, nor may any man chastise a legitimate monarch,
since the prince is naturally supreme, his sovereignty unlimited, and can
be punished by God alone. Conversely, Mariana makes it equally plain
that subjects do have a right to depose or punish a tyrannical ruler, since
man was given the right to choose his own ruler.[41] The authority of the
people, according to Mariana, is "más legítima siempre y mejor que la
del rey tirano."[42] Mariana takes a daring leap by stating that, since
government is a conscious human decision and its formation totally a
result of man's will, man must necessarily also have the right to unmake
it. Since it is man himself who decides upon a superior out of self-
interest, he can then depose the prince later if his self-interest commands
it.[43] His doctrine became a useful weapon with which to justify
resistance to a tyrannical or an allegedly heretical prince. It was thought
at the time—probably erroneously—that the reading of Mariana's *De
Rege* led Ravaillac to assassinate Henry IV of France in 1610.

Mariana, like Bodin, is an advocate of the hereditary right to
kingship since greater respect is naturally given to those of royal
ancestry.[44] It is Mariana's distinct opinion, however, that if a ruler who
attained the throne by hereditary succession chooses to act unwisely and
unbefitting his position, he may be removed from office.[45] Mariana is
"unequivocal, ...on the question of the binding force of law." The king,
in his opinion, is as subject to the law as are the citizens. The laws, he
asserts, can only be sound when the prince himself respects them.[46]
Therefore, according to Mariana's theory, the laws of the state are greater
than the laws of the sovereign. The ruler becomes a tyrant or usurper
when he honors the laws of his ancestors in word but undermines them in
practice. Since the scholastic theory formulated by Thomas Aquinas and

later developed by Vitoria, Suárez and Molina remained unable to provide any real restraints against the abuses of political power that occurred under legitimate sovereignty, Mariana attempts to make the king responsible not merely to God alone, but also to the law of the land and its people.[47] Mariana considers tyranny to be the most evil and prejudicial form of government. A legitimate ruler who allows himself to fall into tyranny must be stopped for the sake of the state.[48]

The defense of the right of resistance and tyrannicide has its origin in the political tradition of the ancient Germanic tribes, and during the Middle Ages the leading exponent of these views was Thomas Aquinas, who stated that "a usurper of political power could be resisted and killed by any individual—force may be met by force".[49] Aquinas, however, does not enter dangerous waters by directing his discourse to the case of a legitimate monarch. Mariana, on the other hand, goes further, extending the right of resistance by the people against even legitimate monarchs whose rule degenerates into tyranny. Such a monarch, however, can be deposed only by public authority.[50] Mariana insists that the tyrannical legitimate monarch must first be warned and then given the opportunity to change his evil ways. If the prince should heed the warning, then no further action need be taken. If, however, he refuses to mend his ways and if there is no other recourse for resolution, it would then be admissible for the commonwealth to retract the grant of power. The estates would be held responsible to declare the tyrant king an outlaw and to direct the contention against him. It is the opinion of Mariana that such an action is lawful since the commonwealth holds the right to restrain or even depose a king who has neglected to fulfill his office in a manner becoming a king. He claims that the rights of the commonwealth are greater than that of the prince since he receives his power from the people.[51] Mariana is even so bold as to admit that if no authorized proceedings have rid the commonwealth of the tyrannical ruler, an individual citizen may take action on his own initiative provided he is authorized by either the estates or some other body of authority. Mariana discusses the value of tyrannicide with hopes that princes, after reading his work, will be educated not to oppress the state. He is most daring when he states that those who fail to behave as just rulers should thus be warned that tyrants are liable to be killed by boldhearted men who wish to defend their rights and the health of their state.[52]

A clear contrast can easily be made again between the political theories of Bodin and Mariana. Bodin, as we have seen, firmly states that the monarch is absolute and that since the monarchy is a gift from God, man does not have the right to chastise or depose even an unjust ruler. If a legitimate sovereign commands that an inappropriate action be fulfilled, the citizen does not need to obey his wish, but this does not permit the active resistance or rebellion of subjects. He believes that the sovereign is absolute and is superior to the state and therefore not bound by the laws of his country. There is no power on earth which is higher than the monarch, and he need not share his power with anyone. Bodin does not place importance upon the consent of the subjects, and he insists that the king should not be subordinate to the authority of the estates. On the other side of the coin, the ideal form of government according to Mariana, as has been stated, is a constitutional monarchy. Mariana views a government of law as superior to the king. The king must be responsible not only to God, as is the view of Bodin, but must also be made accountable to his people and to the law of the land.[53] Mariana diverges from the theory of Bodin in that he believes that the power invested in the prince is derived not directly from God, but from the will of man. Mariana stresses that the subordination of the king to the laws of the community as well as to divine and natural laws is essential if there is to be a healthy monarchy. Seeing the authority of the commonwealth as superior to that of the king, he further differentiates his political thinking from that of Bodin.[54] He believes that the estates should be consulted before any changes are made in the law of succession, since the right to rule depends on the consent of the people. Unlike Bodin, who believes that the king should not be subject to any form of earthly authority, and that the function of the estates is simply to present the humble requests of the citizens, Mariana wants to see the authority of the parliament strengthened and to restore their older and more comprehensive functions.[55] Reacting against the growing absolutism of the Spanish Habsburgs, Mariana emphasizes reliance upon the common sense of mankind, which allows us to "distinguish right from wrong" and which does not allow us to disregard the misconduct of a tyrannical ruler.[56]

NOTES

[1] Jean Bodin, *The Six Bookes of a Commonweale*, a facsimile reprint of the English translation of *La République* of 1606, ed. Kenneth Douglas McRae (Cambridge: Harvard UP, 1962), pp. 159–160.

[2] McRae, Introduction to Bodin, *The Six Bookes*, p. A14.

[3] Bodin, pp. 88 and 106.

[4] Bodin, p. 153.

[5] Bodin, pp. 92 and 104–106.

[6] McRae, Introduction to Bodin, *The Six Bookes*, pp. A15–16; see also Bodin, pp. 174–175.

[7] Bodin, p. 222; see also McRae, Introduction to Bodin, *The Six Bookes*, pp. A15–A16.

[8] McRae, Introduction to Bodin, *The Six Bookes*, p. A16.

[9] Bodin, *The Six Bookes*, pp. 92–93 and pp. 106–107; see also McRae, Introduction to Bodin, *The Six Bookes*, p. A16.

[10] McRae, Introduction to Bodin, *The Six Bookes*, p. A16; see also Bodin, *The Six Bookes*, pp. 110–111.

[11] McRae, Introduction to Bodin, *The Six Bookes*, p. A16; see also Bodin, *The Six Bookes*, pp. 177–179 and 665.

[12] Bodin, *The Six Bookes*, p. 8.

[13] Bodin, *The Six Bookes*, pp. 20–21.

[14] Beatrice Reynolds, Introduction to her translation, under the title of *Method for the Easy Comprehension of History*, of Bodin's, *Methodus ad facilem historiarum cognitionem* (New York: Octagon Books, Inc., 1966), p. xvii.

[15] Bodin, *Method for the Easy Comprehension of History*, trans. Beatrice Reynolds (New York: Octagon Books, Inc., 1966), p. 271.

[16] W.H. Greenleaf, " Bodin and the Idea of Order," in *Jean Bodin*, (Munich: Verlag C.H. Beck, 1973), p. 33; see also Bodin, *The Six Bookes*, p. 717.

[17] Bodin, *The Six Bookes*, pp. 20–21; see also Reynolds, Introduction to Bodin, *Method*, p. xvi, and Bodin, *Method*, p. 277.

[18] Bodin, *Method*, p. 268; see also Bodin, *The Six Bookes*, pp. 793–794; see also Greenleaf, p. 27.

[19] Bodin, *Method*, p. 271; see also Greenleaf, pp. 28–29.

[20] Bodin, *The Six Bookes*, pp. 793–794.

[21] Bodin, *Method*, pp. 276–277.

[22] Bodin, *The Six Bookes*, p. 313.

[23] Bodin, *Method*, p. 289; see also Bodin, *The Six Bookes*, p. 215.

[24] Bodin, *The Six Bookes*, p. 212.

[25] Bodin, *Method*, p. 290.

[26] Bodin, *Method*, p. 290.

[27] Reynolds, Introduction to Bodin, *Method*, p. xviii.

[28] Bodin, *The Six Bookes*, p. 313.

[29] Bodin, *The Six Bookes*, pp. 218–219.

[30] Bodin, *The Six Bookes*, p. 222.

[31] Bodin, *The Six Bookes*, pp. 221–222 and 225.

[32] Bodin, *The Six Bookes*, pp. 95–98.

[33] Bodin, *The Six Bookes*, p. 325.

[34] Juan de Mariana, "Del Rey y de la Institución Real," in *Biblioteca de Autores Españoles*, vol. 31(Madrid: M. Rivadeneyra, 1854), pp. 485–488; see also Guenter Lewy, *Constitutionalism and Statecraft during the Golden Age of Spain: A Study of the Political Philosophy of Juan de Mariana, S.J.* (Geneva: Librairie E. Droz, 1960), pp. 66–67.

[35] Lewy, p. 28.

[36] Mariana, pp. 467–468; see also Lewy, pp. 45–46.

[37] Mariana, pp. 467–468; see also Lewy, pp. 37–38 and 43–44.

[38] Mariana, pp. 467–468; see also Lewy, p. 39.

[39] Lewy, p. 45.

[40] Lewy, p. 45.

[41] Mariana, p. 481.

[42] Mariana, p. 482.

[43] Lewy, p. 45, (Lewy explains that Mariana attempts to prove the right of the people to choose their rulers in the *History* by describing the turbulent times at the accession of John II of Castile in 1407. Lewy quotes a nobleman in Mariana as saying: "Through the consent of people kingships can be changed, new kings can be instituted which is proven by the nature of the royal power: that which originated in the will of the people can, if circumstances require it, be transferred to others" (citing Juan de Mariana, *Historiae de rebus Hispaniae*, lib. XIX, chap. XV).

[44] Mariana, pp. 472–475; see also Lewy, p. 54.

[45] Mariana, p. 481; see also Lewy, p. 45.

[46] Mariana, p. 478; see also Lewy, p. 60.

[47] Mariana, pp. 485–488; see also Lewy, pp. 64–65.

[48] Mariana, p. 477 and 482; see also Lewy, p. 68.

[49] Lewy, p. 76.

[50] Mariana, pp. 479–483.

[51] Mariana, pp. 485–488.

[52] Mariana, pp. 479–485; see also Lewy, pp. 72–74.

[53] Lewy, p. 65.
[54] Lewy, p. 66.
[55] Mariana, pp. 488–491; see also Lewy, p. 84.
[56] Lewy, p. 78.

CHAPTER II
THE PRIVADO

The *valido* played so prominent a role in seventeenth-century government that he could not be overlooked by any political theorist. Although Charles V and Philip II governed with the aid of the secretaries of state, during the reign of Philip III these secretaries lost their importance and gave way to a single favorite minister of the king, the *privado*.[1] It can then be said that the reign of Philip III marked the beginning of a distinct change from the more personal rule of Philip II to a government run almost single-handedly by the king's favorite. This man, more than anyone else, enjoyed royal friendship and confidence. The figure of the *valido* can be seen not as a new form of secretary of state, but as a more powerful and authoritative figure because of his close relationship with the king and his consequent powerful influence over the monarch and his decisions. There was a succession of favorites until the end of the seventeenth century. It was not just Spain, however, that fell into the adoption of a royal favorite who would handle the responsibilities of government; she followed the same pattern as did other countries in the seventeenth century. France also gave importance to this person, who assumed almost autonomous control over state affairs. Cardinal Richelieu played as important a role in seventeenth-century France as the Count-Duke of Olivares did during the same period in Spanish history. J. H. Elliott examines these two political figures and compares and contrasts them in his study *Richelieu and Olivares* (Cambridge, 1984).

Typical characteristics of the figure of the *valido* stressed by analysts of the day include the following: The favorite must share a long-standing, loyal friendship with the monarch which has its beginnings even before the king takes the throne. The king should feel a total sense of confidence in the ability of this man to aid him with any matters of state which may arise. As a result of the royal confidence enjoyed by the *valido* he will have the authority to intervene directly in the government of the monarchy. He is generally a very ambitious man who thrives on the feeling of power and control with which he is entrusted. Futhermore, he is usually a man of the high nobility, since it would seem likely that only a nobleman would have the necessary education, knowledge, and family connections to aid the king with important matters of state. [2]

At this point it is opportune to consider the reasons why the *valido* evolved. One explanation lies in the character of the individual king.[3] For example, if a sovereign were of weak character and lacked the necessary diligence, discipline and political aptitude to govern the country on his own, he might find such a willing and experienced servant of the state a very comforting assistant to have around. He might even rely on the confident and authoritative favorite to be the sole voice of power. Francisco Tomás y Valiente offers still another explanation, namely, that the favorite's existence was due to the astuteness of certain men who were ambitious and cunning enough to scheme and plot for the power to control the government.[4] Further, if the king was viewed as a divinely ordained being, viceroy of God , he could never be made the object of blame or attack. The royal favorite, then, would always remain the blamable party for any wrong committed during the reign since untouchability and blamelessness are attributes of the divinely ordained king. The *valido* in this way then acted as the scapegoat for the errors perpetrated by the monarch.[5] Now let us consider some of the factors in the power and authority of the royal favorite. There was, as we have said, a firm collaboration established between the king and his favorite. These men shared a special bond of friendship which is illustrated in many of the plays examined in this study. The trust that the monarch placed in his favorite was so complete that the *valido* actually became the executor of royal authority and as such necessarily was to be respected and obeyed by all subjects of the state. The favorite was seen as an agent influencing all royal decisions because of the constant close contact between minister and king. The reigns of Philip III and Philip IV of Spain were prime breeding grounds for the *valido* since both monarchs lacked the self-confidence and diligence necessary for the proper government of Spain. The feeble character of both these sovereigns (most particularly of Philip III) was compensated for by the assertiveness and manipulation of their favorites, upon whom they leaned constantly for direction.

Unfortunately for the favorite, although the support and appreciation he received from the sovereign was almost always apparent in the gifts, titles and grants that he received from royal as well as other hands, he was not always popular among the nobility and people. Many detested the person of the royal favorite since his very presence was considered as a direct contradiction to the already generally accepted theory of the absolute monarchy, in which the supreme authority of power is vested only in the king. An all-encompassing power manifest in the person of the *valido* thus was felt to be unacceptable. The arrogant nobility was often forced to bow to the will of the *privado* and thus bitterly resented him. The old grandees and aspiring nobles often felt irritated by, and distrustful and jealous of, the favorite, who seemed to be gaining all the rewards as he climbed the ladder of success. The feeling of jealousy seemed to spread like wildfire to all spheres of the state, from the nobility to the populace, with the favorite then victimized by their discontent and slander. Even the townspeople hated the *valido* because of his vast power.[6]

Undeniably the favorite's position at Court was an enviable one to many,[7] but, however desirable his post may have appeared to others, it was an exhausting job for the minister himself. He was constantly opposed by nobles and politicians, many of whom were more interested in their own personal gain than in the betterment of their country. Another difficulty which faced the royal favorite was the popular assumption that the *valido* had gained the favor of the king through sinister means. For example, in January of 1625, when Don Gaspar de Guzmán, Conde de Olivares, was awarded a dukedom, many of his enemies were outraged, finding Philip's confidence in his favorite to be incomprehensible. These enemies attributed this royal confidence in Olivares to the practice of magical arts. As early as 1622 stories had circulated about the magical potions which Olivares supposedly administered to the young king in order to retain his favor. It is no wonder that Olivares rejected the term *privado*, preferring to call himself the king's "faithful minister." [8]

Political writers and thinkers of the seventeenth century spoke and wrote openly concerning their opinions of the role of the royal favorite. Fundamentally, the political literature was pedagogical and didactic, offering many suggestions as to the ideal virtues of the perfect royal favorite. On many occasions the writers felt that the role of the *valido* was that of the education of the king. The favorite should be a living model of virtue for the king to emulate.[9] Many believed it just for a king to have a loyal and true friend whom he could turn to in times of great stress and need and agreed that the favorite should be someone with whom the sovereign could advantageously share his most intimate feelings. Those who were not totally averse to the presence of a royal favorite insisted nonetheless that his authority must always be subordinate to that of the king. Their only wish was to limit the power of the *valido* because they recognized the benefits of his presence. All agreed that the sovereignty of the king is indivisible and inalienable. In general, the majority of the writers judged that there was a positive need for the *valido* as a true and loyal friend to the king, and therefore they were tolerant of his position.[10]

There were, however, some who remained adamantly opposed to *valido*(s), believing the government to be most effective only if the monarch were to rule on his own as Philip II had done.[11] Fray Juan de Santamaría was the leading advocate and spokesman of the anti-favorite faction; during the reign of Philip III, he spoke out openly against the system of government dominated by a single, all-powerful *valido*. He felt strongly that it was the king's duty to attend personally to serious matters of state, following the advice of good councillors. He insisted that Castile had found itself in such a poor state because the king was un-aware of what was occurring in his own realms. In the simplest of terms, what Fray Juan de Santamaría was struggling for was a return to a more personal kingship.[12]

The succession of *valido*(s), which continued late into the seven-teenth century, began with the Duke of Lerma, don Francisco Gómez de Sandoval y Rojas, whose position as the favorite of King Philip III lasted twenty years (1598–1618).[13] After his fall from power, his son, the Duke of Uceda, immediately took over government matters until the death of this king (1621).[14] Philip III, a weak king, proved to be a dis-grace to his people. He was known to have been stricken with guilt and regret upon his deathbed for not having taken more personal control of government.[15] When Philip IV, his son, acceded to the throne, he was determined not to rely on the authority of a favorite and thus avoid the repetition of the mistake of his unpopular father. Since the king was only sixteen years of age, don Baltasar de Zúñiga was asked to aid the young monarch but was never referred to as the monarch's *valido*.[16] Upon the death of Zúñiga in 1622, don Gaspar de Guzmán, Count of Olivares, and Zúñiga's nephew, took control of state affairs and became the king's royal favorite.[17] This relationship lasted a bit longer than twenty years, since he did not fall from power until January of 1643. Luis Méndez de Haro, nephew of Olivares, who took over governmental operations until he died five years later, prudently rejected the title of the king's *valido* or even that of first minister.[18] Olivares was truly the last of the great *privado*(s).

It is fitting then, that the figure of don Gaspar de Guzmán, the Count of Olivares, be treated at some length in order to see how the most famous *privado* functioned. (For the purposes of this study, he is also the most significant *privado* because he had been a fellow student of Alarcón's at the University of Salamanca in 1601–1602.) He began working in the Court of Philip III as one of the attendants in the chamber of the young ten-year-old prince, the future Philip IV. He used this post as a stepping stone for future advancement, patiently awaiting the appropriate moment in which to take control. In 1622, only one year after Philip IV had inherited the throne, Olivares was appointed Master of the Horse, which like his other court position, would keep him in close contact with the king. Olivares finally came to power by strategically plotting his way. He and his uncle, don Baltasar de Zúñiga, who in April of 1621 was chosen to help the young king Philip with the government of the Monarchy, worked together carefully picking and choosing the men to work under Olivares. It was these hand-picked men, known as Olivares's *hechuras* (creatures), who later managed affairs of state under the directing hands of Olivares.[19]

Upon the death of Zúñiga in 1622, Olivares became virtually the supreme governor of the monarchy, and, although he preferred the term "minister",[20] he was generally acknowledged as the king's new favorite. The term *privado* or *valido* had a distinctly pejorative interpretation among the citizens of Spain, who were totally disillusioned with the dependence of Philip III on the Duke of Lerma. It appeared, however, that Olivares did not, like Lerma, assume the post for reasons of self-interest or greed. He accepted few gifts from admirers and was certainly not overpaid for the endless number of hours that he devoted to state business.[21] He took a seat on the Council of State as the first minister of the Crown and immediately proclaimed the need for restoration of old moral values together with discipline and austerity. During his stay in office, he was known, unlike Lerma, to be hard-working and energetic, although he was unpopular amongst the Spanish nobility and other court officials who saw that their own interests were being threatened by Olivares.[22] Nevertheless, he worked with undeniable good intentions for the betterment of his country, no matter how frustrated, fruitless and unsuccessful his attempts may have proven to be.

Like Fray Juan de Santamaría and Bodin and Mariana before him,
Olivares firmly believed that a young monarch must receive the proper
training to be able to govern his country more personally. He took it
upon himself to instruct the young Philip in the ways befitting a king and
lectured him on the responsibility of kings to govern personally. He
may even "have placed a copy of Santamaría's book [*República y policía
cristiana* (1615)] in his hands."[23] Further, to be a great monarch Philip
must not only possess the necessary political knowledge to govern but
must also be taught to have an appreciation for art and music. Olivares
therefore became the personal tutor of the young king, guiding and instructing him as to the duties and obligations of an ideal sovereign.[24]

There existed a real bond between Olivares and his king. It can be
explained by the fact that they had very different, yet complementary,
personalities. Philip lacked political training, and more importantly, self-
confidence. "The king's persistent doubts about his own abilities, his
need for someone to whom he could turn for advice and reassurance, and
the sheer quantity of paper-work involved in the government of the
Spanish Monarchy, made it improbable that he could dispense with the
services of an intimate counselor."[25] Philip also enjoyed the pleasures of
hunting and, when tired of the tasks of kingship, headed for the hunting-
fields.[26] Olivares, on the other hand, was a domineering sort who thrived
under intense pressure. The work this man could tackle, together with
the almost total lack of relaxation he permitted himself, required almost
superhuman energy. He was often frustrated by others who were, more
often than not, less dedicated to the Crown.[27]

Olivares was a great reforming minister, at least in terms of intention
if not of achievement. He proclaimed the need for a total restoration
program for Castile. Don Rodrigo Calderón, a favorite of the Lerma
regime, was beheaded in the Plaza Mayor on 21 October, 1621, as a symbol of the cleansing and regeneration which was promised under the
reign of Philip IV. Unfortunately, however, Calderón died in such a
dignified manner that the people began to view him as a martyr rather
than a criminal, and the new regime under Olivares did not receive a favorable judgment on its decision to execute him.[28]

Olivares's long-term goal was the restoration of the reputation of the
king of Spain, the unification of the territories, the economic revival of
Castile, and the spread of the Catholic religion. He saw the need for
stronger kingship, which would then lead to a more complete national

regeneration. The traditional approach of Olivares is reflected in "The Great Memorial," dated 25 December, 1624, written by Olivares with the purpose of educating the king. The king is seen as the embodiment of public authority, and Olivares explains that the dignity and authority of the king had to be restored in order to achieve a healthy and well-balanced nation, as it was in the time of Ferdinand and Isabel.[29] His was also the traditionalist view that an authoritative figure was needed to control disorder and decay. He, like Jean Bodin, believed that first and foremost the preeminence of the king was the essential criterion in achieving a more balanced and healthy body politic.[30]

NOTES

[1] Francisco Tomás y Valiente, *Los validos en la monarquía española del siglo XVII* (Valencia: Siglo Veintiuno Editores, 1982), pp. 52–53.

[2] Tomás y Valiente, pp. 30, 54, 114.

[3] Tomás y Valiente, p. 34.

[4] Tomás y Valiente, p. 34.

[5] Tomás y Valiente, pp. 65–67 and 81.

[6] Tomás y Valiente, pp. 108,117–118,120.

[7] Tomás y Valiente, p. 117.

[8] J. H. Elliott, *The Count-Duke of Olivares. The Statesman in an Age of Decline* (New Haven and London: Yale UP, 1986), p. 169.

[9] Tomás y Valiente, pp. 123–126.

[10] Tomás y Valiente, pp. 131–143.

[11] Tomás y Valiente, p. 143.

[12] Tomás y Valiente, pp. 143–146; see also Elliott, *The Count-Duke*, pp. 102 and 170.

[13] Tomás y Valiente, p. 7.

[14] Tomás y Valiente, pp. 8–9.

[15] Elliott, *The Count-Duke*, p. 4; see also Tomás y Valiente, p. 9.

[16] Tomás y Valiente, pp. 9–11.

[17] Tomás y Valiente, p. 13.

[18] Tomás y Valiente, p. 17.

[19] Elliott, *The Count-Duke*, pp. 136–137.

[20] Elliott, *The Count-Duke*, p. 169.

[21] Elliott, *The Count-Duke*, pp. 104 and 533.

[22] Elliott, *The Count-Duke*, pp. 108, 311, 478–479, 557.

[23] Elliott, *The Count-Duke*, p. 102.
[24] Elliott, *The Count-Duke*, pp. 172–178.
[25] Elliott, *The Count-Duke*, p. 179.
[26] Elliott, *The Count-Duke*, p. 103.
[27] Elliott, *The Count-Duke*, pp. 290–295.
[28] Elliott, *The Count-Duke*, pp. 107–108.
[29] Elliott, *The Count-Duke*, pp. 179–182.
[30] Elliott, *The Count-Duke*, pp. 178–202.

CHAPTER III
A NATION'S DECLINE

The reign of Philip II (1556–1598) marked the beginning of Spanish social and economic decline. Taxes tripled during the 1560's and 1570's and were hardly able to keep up with the rapidly growing inflation in the 1580's and 1590's. In order for the Crown to meet the inflation costs, it was forced to sell off to the wealthy and privileged many lands and villages under royal jurisdiction. It was also compelled to sell off large tracts of land that traditionally had "free-use privileges" for the public. These pieces of land played an integral part in the economic welfare of the townspeople and peasants alike. By the end of the sixteenth century, an oligarchy of wealthy landowners had been formed who could take advantage of the farming peasants by demanding an excessive payment for the use of their land. It was this oligarchy which, later in the seventeenth century, during the reign of Philip IV, proved to be more interested in the passive enjoyment of its incoming wealth than in the active and advantageous management of its money for the sake of the entire country and its population.[1]

Another economic strain in the later sixteenth century was caused by the massive infringement upon the pasture-land of the sheep farmers by the crop farmers. Wool was the major source of Castilian textile production, and it was also a major source of exports for Spain. However, there was also a constant pressure to produce enough cereals to provide for Spain's expanding population which had reached its limits by the 1570's. Both the sheep farmers and the arable farmers met insuperable pressures. While the sheep industry was being squeezed out, the peasant farmers who "had taken out loans in order to finance their cultivation of new land" were also faced with impossible loan payments. As land became scarcer and the rents higher, farmers' profits dropped rapidly, and an increasing number of peasants found it difficult to meet their interest payments. These peasants were also burdened with "seigneurial, ecclesiastical and royal dues." As their debts reached impossible proportions, many of these farmers chose to escape their farm lands searching for greater security in the cities. The rapid disappearance of agricultural laborers put a great stress on the Spanish economy.[2] Nor was the weather conducive to rural prosperity. The summers of the 1590's produced a famine situation caused by years of excessive rain, which in consequence meant many poor harvests. Another element of bad luck for Castile was the plague of 1596–1602, which eliminated approximately ten percent of its total population. Castile was faced with a "long phase of demographic stagnation and recession that would continue until the later years of the seventeenth century."[3] It must be emphasized, therefore, that by the end of the reign of Philip II, regardless of the fact that he exemplified the ideal of personal leadership, Spain was already in trouble. Philip II, in his final years of rule, found the conservation of his world-wide Monarchy impossible to maintain. "The revolt of the Netherlands, the war with England, the intervention in the civil wars in France, had all taken a heavy toll of the Monarchy's resources, and imposed enormous strains on Castile."[4]

Philip III's reign (1598–1621) was forced to bear the consequences of past military campaigns, and pessimism grew concerning the course of events in central Europe, which might require Spain's military intervention and further devastating expenditures. The Protestant and anti-Habsburg forces in Bohemia were increasing in strength and proved to be an enormous threat to Spanish control. As Elliott states, Spain was pressed by a number of problems: "the enemies of the House of Austria—the forces of international Calvinism, the Venetians and the Dutch—were engaged in a vast conspiracy to secure its overthrow."[5] Military intervention in Bohemia is what Zúñiga and ambassador Oñate advised in order to regain Spain's reputation. Zúñiga regarded reputation as not only an end in itself, but as an instrument for the conduct of foreign policy and as "an essential component of power."[6] The force of the military seemed to be the only defense left for Spain if the great monarchical empire established by Philip II was to be preserved.[7] Zúñiga also argued that England had to be "neutralized" in order to isolate the problem with the Dutch. English neutralization would mean that the Spanish could better restrain the Protestant princes and especially Frederick V, the Elector Palatine in Germany.[8]

Philip III's ministers also had to decide whether to prolong the Twelve Years' Truce with the Dutch (signed in 1609), or to enter into an all-out war. Dutch participation in European and overseas trade caused economic hardships both for Spain and Portugal. The invasion of the Dutch into the Pacific and Indian oceans during the years of truce after

1609 was of deep concern to the Spanish government, not only because of the decline in the trade and wealth of Portugal and her merchants, but also because of the tension which that decline caused in the already fragile relationship between Portugal and Castile. In the spring of 1619, Philip III found the Portuguese disillusioned with the union of the Crowns of Castile and Portugal achieved in 1580, and especially troubled by the fact that the Spanish Crown was unable to protect their overseas possessions. The Councils of Portugal and the Indies pressed hard for the resumption of war, believing that the Dutch might put an end to interests overseas if they were confronted with the possibility of war with Spain.[9] Spain was faced with this dilemma knowing that the cost of war was far too great for an already weak economy. "The treasury was empty, the nobility indebted, the peasantry poverty-stricken."[10] The only money which remained was that of the Church; and, however painful that might be, the Church's money was needed to maintain Spain's defenses against Protestantism and Islam. Zúñiga recommended to Philip III to capitalize on Spain's ecclesiastical wealth, even if this meant "melting down the communion cups."[11]

Zúñiga and Oñate, together with Archduke Albert in Brussels, brother to the late Emperor and committed to the family cause, urged on Philip III the necessity for large-scale intervention in the Palatinate against the Protestant rebels in the Habsburg lands so as to lessen the pressure on the Habsburg Emperor, prohibit Protestant forces from occupying Alsace, encourage Maximilian of Bavaria to assist Emperor Ferdinand in Bohemia, and force the Dutch into agreeing to a "continuation of the truce on more favourable terms."[12] The terms which would have pleased these military advisors were that the Dutch would allow "freedom of worship" for their Catholics, abandon trade with the Indies, and re-open the river Scheldt to trade by lifting the blockade of Antwerp.[13] On 9 May, 1620, Philip III officially authorized the invasion of the Palatinate. Luckily for Spain the Habsburg and Catholic cause was triumphant in Germany,[14] but the problem of what to do with the Dutch was still unsettled and the truce had almost expired. On 31 March, 1621, the very day of Philip III's death, the attempts to secure a continuation of the truce with the Dutch on more advantageous terms for Spain proved futile.[15]

On 22 April, the new king, Philip IV, was crowned, and he approved the decision to enter into war in Flanders. "The Twelve Years' Truce

expired formally on the tenth day of the new reign." This decision led
Spain into what would be another "twenty-seven years of warfare with
the Dutch." The resumption of war in the Netherlands became one of
the chief charges against the Olivares administration.[16] The expiration
of the truce with the Netherlands imposed a burden on the taxpayers in
order to support the heavy military and naval expenditures that had been
incurred. The treasury had so completely drained its funds that in July,
1621, the Council of Finance reported that it was impossible for the
Crown to meet its outstanding debts to its bankers. It was even necessary
to expend anticipated funds in order to meet each year's expenses.[17]

Decades of deficit financing had given rise to the massive indebtedness of the Crown. Continuing into the reign of Philip IV, this deficit
financing forced the diversion of capital from more fruitful forms of investment and created economic chaos by distorting the true financial picture of the government.[18] The easiest way for the Crown to handle its
internal financing was to manufacture a copper coinage called *vellón*.
This tampering with the currency, initiated by Philip III, occurred even
more frequently under Philip IV. This overcoined and overrated currency became the main medium of exchange in circulation in Castile
around 1622–23, but was only serviceable in Spain.[19]

The sales tax, as well as the king's usual revenues, were never sufficient to pay debts of the current year or the debts accruing from preceding years. All revenues, therefore, went to pay the interest on sums not
paid in previous years. There were even taxes levied on basic domestic
goods such as wine, olive oil, vinegar and meat. Financial problems
were compounded by the fall in the value of silver remittances from the
Indies. For the sake of comparison, in the opening years of Philip III's
reign, the Crown could depend on some two million ducats of American
silver a year. In 1615 and 1616, this sum dropped drastically to one
million ducats. By 1620, this figure was reduced again to a mere
845,000 ducats. The American viceroyalties of Mexico and Peru became
increasingly less reliant on Spain for trade, turning to other European
markets for their needs. The cost of silver production in the New World
climbed as a result of a lack of mercury needed for the refining process.
The drop of silver remittances in the last years of Philip III's reign was
likely due to the fact that the American viceroys decided to hold on to
silver in order to strengthen coastal defenses against the Dutch. Since
American silver constituted a large portion of the Crown's annual

income, this decline in remittances was a great worry to Spain. What made it all the more serious was that the Crown's Genoese bankers would accept payment only in silver and not in *vellón*. Because of the scarcity of silver, Philip IV was forced to continue the impounding of otherwise consigned silver for his own use, and the burden of Crown indebtedness increased.[20]

High interest rates for government loans was also another cause of financial strain for the entire nation. The interest earned on government loans was higher than the profits generated by the goods and services produced by the farmers and manufacturers, a situation which only benefitted the financiers. The result was that people then tried to survive on their investment income instead of using their capital for more nationally productive forms of investment. The economic decline of the kingdom can be attributed to the constant pressure on the Crown's treasury, which, though begun decades earlier, accelerated under the Olivares administration. The economic stress felt by the entire nation had drastic effects upon the people of Castile. The ever increasing amount of poverty in Spain, for example, became a real problem as economic conditions continued to decline. Among those who devoted special attention to the problem of the poor during the reigns of Philip II and III, no man was more consistently dedicated than Cristóbal Pérez de Herrera (1558–1625), a medical doctor, politician and poet, who witnessed the beginning of the decline during the reign of Philip II, lived through the terrible years of Philip III, and even survived to see the beginning years of the Zúñiga-Olivares administration. He dedicated his life to the aid of the poor, who he felt were victims of the decline. His outstanding reputation earned him the unanimous respect of his contemporaries. Juan Ruiz de Alarcón was certainly among the men who admired the work of this great humanitarian.

In the year 1618, Pérez de Herrera's *Proverbios morales y consejos cristianos* appeared; among the laudatory verses by many authors printed in the first pages of the book were included two quintillas by Alarcón. At the end of the book, Pérez de Herrera published "catorce proposiciones que aparecen ser muy importantes para el bien y descanso de estos reinos," propositions which set forth many of his suggestions for the betterment of Spain's economic condition. These fourteen proposals, apparently sent to the Cortes in 1619, anticipated the proposals of the reform Junta of 1623 under the Olivares administration, which dealt with many

of the same issues. [21]   I shall treat Pérez de Herrera's proposals in detail
because many of them find their way into Alarcón's political plays.

First, Pérez de Herrera expressed a concern for the increasing number of false beggars in Spain. Legitimate ones, he argued, should be
given food and shelter, and the sons of beggars should be taught a useful
trade, which would be far more beneficial to the nation than teaching
them grammar and Latin. Vagabonds in the kingdom should be made to
do useful tasks, especially in the areas of farming and serving on the
galleys.

He was opposed to the excessive amount of money spent on clothing,
servants and food. He suggested that *premáticas* (edicts) be issued in
order to prevent such unnecessary spending and insisted that the implementation of these edicts be rigorously supervised. What would be the
purpose of the edicts if nothing was done to insure their enforcement?

Farming was also an important issue to Pérez de Herrera, who felt
that farmers should be encouraged by reducing their tax load. Flour,
wheat and seeds should be stored in order to prevent scarcity during
years of drought. Livestock was another target area of Pérez de Herrera's
proposals. People should be encouraged to raise more cattle and to
construct winter shelter for the animals, as in Germany and other places.

Another important proposal was the encouragement of trade, and the
seas must first be safe against pirates and enemy ships in order for trade
to flourish. Duty and excise taxes (*alcabalas* and *millones*) should also
be reduced so as to encourage trade. Foreign merchants should be permitted to enter the kingdom, marry and reside with their families in order
to keep the money that these merchants earned within Spain's confines.
He wanted to see annuities (*juros* and *censos*) increased so that people
should have money to invest in activities such as commerce or the pur-
chase of cattle and wheat-bearing land.

Attempts should also be made to repopulate Spain with more serviceable people, perhaps those who were at one time exiled from Spain
(an obvious reference to the Jews). Vagabonds, *beatas,* and hermits
should be made to work. Marriage should also be encouraged as a way
to increase population, and in order to keep population up in the towns
and villages, the feudal lords of towns should reside in them rather than
at Court and they should treat the peasants well.

Rivers should be made navigable, and many trees should be planted
with good irrigation systems maintained. Prices of necessities should be

brought down and usurers banished. The price of silk should be regulated; and cities such as Segovia and others with a tradition of clothmaking should set up their own textile-weaving industry, so that cloth need not be imported from all over the world.

He was also concerned about the amount of silver and gold leaving the country and considered the prevention of the drain of precious metals of much importance. At the same time the quantity of debased *vellón* coins should be reduced.

In addition, Pérez de Herrera proposed to reduce the number of legal parasites such as notaries (*escribanos*). People holding these useless jobs should be redirected to more profitable occupations such as those of soldiers, traders, artisans, farmers and cattle raisers.

The number of monasteries and convents should be limited because if their numbers increased, not only the new foundations but the older established ones would be impoverished. Convents, however, should exist where poor noblewomen and women who ask for divorce might be kept decently and without scandal. The number of teachers and schools of grammar was another concern because the common people, who acquire a little Latin out of convenience, become priests and monks instead of continuing the tradition of their fathers as farmers. As a result of the teaching of grammar to the common people, the farms were not being cultivated for the benefit of the nation.

Types of taxes and their collection should be reconsidered, for the expense of collection was often greater than returns to the treasury. The king must also reduce his personal expenses in order to pay the salaries of loyal ministers and servants promptly.

Lastly, he repeated his insistence that the number of edicts be reduced at the same time that their enforcement was rigorously pursued.[22]

The most famous of Pérez de Herrera's works, *Discursos del amparo de los legítimos pobres y reducción de los fingidos: y de la fundación y principio de los albergues destos reinos, y amparo de la milicia dellos*, was published in 1598 during the reign of Philip II, and dedicated to Prince Philip, the future Philip III. Pérez de Herrera proposed to unmask the false beggars who usurped the Christian charity of the citizens of Spain, and to offer reform measures which would help the living conditions of the honest poor. This problem of the poor became a center of great ideological conflicts in the sixteenth century; by the middle of that century, the movement against beggary had gained considerable force.

Pérez de Herrera was a witness himself to the evils and injustices of poverty as the examining physician (*protomédico*) assigned to survey conditions in the galleys before he was promoted to the post of court doctor under Philip II.[23]

Poverty and its resultant beggary and vagabondism were a problem shared by all countries of Western Europe since the beginning of the fourteenth century. Spain, however, was suffering from a particularly acute case. In the decade of 1521–1531 there was a sudden upsurge in the number of vagrants of Spain. The supremacy of the "chivalric" mentality, which honored idleness over the work of the artisan, was a major factor in the increased beggary in the Republic. This same mentality was also to blame for the decay of Castile's industry through the lack of manual labor. Cavillac points his finger at the aristocratic disdain for manual labor in general and for the aversion to "productive" enterprises. It was "la teoría aristocrática del menosprecio por el trabajo manual, que infamaba a quien ejercía un arte mecánica." [24]

Another cause of the increased poverty level in Spain was, as we have seen, the ever growing number of peasant farmers who chose the idle life of begging rather than fighting the impossible economic odds that faced them. The years 1592–1600 marked the height of inflationary price increases caused by the influx of American silver. The beggar became the symbol of the destitute man alienated by the Genoese banking aristocracy. In *Amparo de pobres*, it is these people whom Herrera describes as beggars of good and honorable formation, "de buena gente y limpia," victims of the social and economic structure.[25]

As prices also continued to rise at a steady rate, the bourgeoisie was inevitably discouraged, and they also lost their initiative. The depression of 1596–1607 can be seen as the sign and portent of the destruction of the bourgeoisie in Burgos and Sevilla.[26] The *pícaro* was the victim of the great disparity in society between the beggars and the idle aristocracy. He was unable to incorporate himself into the nobility, and with the collapse of the bourgeoisie, he was forced to live as a half-outsider.

Pérez de Herrera also tried to assist the poor by advocating many reform measures. He was much influenced by the work of Juan Luis Vives (1492–1540), the Valencian humanist who was self-exiled to Flanders for fear of the Inquisition.[27] In his work "De subventione pauperum," published in 1526, Vives advocated improving the conditions of the poor in a rational way. Instead of the old attitude of blind charity for the sake of appearance, he suggested a new attitude of reform with the benefit of the state in mind.[28] For example, Vives believed in obligatory work for all.[29] As measures for reform, he suggested instituting hospitals where orphan children could be raised and where the blind and mentally and physically ill could go for help.[30]

Pérez de Herrera, influenced by the ideas of Luis Vives, likewise argued for improving the living conditions of the poor in a rational way. As a doctor, he detested the sickness and the decay that increased poverty was bringing to Spain. The idleness of the poor was also a fundamental problem. Again influenced by humanist thinking, he saw this idleness as the root of evil action. Like Vives, he believed in obligatory work for all,[31] as is evident in so many of the reform proposals studied above. Following Luis Vives's suggestions, he took action to find work for all beggars to help the community's efforts for reform. He founded a hospital to care for the sick and needy[32] and founded shelters (*albergues*) where the sick could go to receive proper medical attention. The legitimate poor were also given religious insignias to wear so that there could be more control of false beggary.[33] Pérez de Herrera helped to alter drastically the meaning of the word "charity," which, because of his reform program, was more gratifying since it dealt with the legitimate poor.[34]

This humanitarian doctor also encouraged enthusiasm for the military life. He was awake to the current problem of the lack of good soldiers. As a soldier himself for twelve years, Pérez de Herrera was well aware of the perils that awaited them at every corner. Therefore, soldiers should be well compensated for the dangers they encounter for the sake of their country. Special awards and benefits should be given to soldiers; even churches were encouraged to give generously to the military. It was his intention to raise not only the standards of living of the soldiers, but also to enhance their reputation, so that many more people would find the military life appealing and thus improve the national defense.[35]

The work of Pérez de Herrera during the sixteenth and early part of the seventeenth centuries was the source of many of the recommendations later offered by Olivares in his struggle to save his country from ruination. The Junta de Reformación (1623) under his administration proposed many of the same ideas. Both Pérez de Herrera and Olivares, for example, were rational thinkers and saw the importance of work for all men. Olivares attempted to expel from the towns and villages vagrants who were idle beggars and had nothing to offer the Republic. He was also, like Pérez de Herrera, sympathetic to the poor, and felt that many were victims of a misguided government. Olivares was also concerned about the needs of abandoned and orphaned children. Both men believed that they should be offered the proper training for jobs that would benefit the country.

Needless to say, by the time of Philip IV's accession to the throne, reform measures were desperately needed, and the king's *valido* more than anyone else, attempted to push them forward. The formation of the Junta de Reformación, composed of ministers appointed by Olivares himself, was one of the first acts of his administration. His aim was to raise the standards of public manners and morals and to offer proposals for the reform of the failing economy. This recourse to juntas, as has already been indicated, was really nothing new in the history of the Spanish administration. To repeat, under Philip III the creation of committees of ministers was a common practice.[36] Olivares, however, gave these juntas a new meaning. He was in actuality setting up an alternative administration outside the royal councils which would give him an edge in the decision-making of the government. Olivares was highly criticized as a result of these juntas. His enemies' concern was that this hand-picked committee of six to eight men gave Olivares even more controlling power. He was the direct executor of the royal will, as were other royal ministers of other monarchies; the correspondence was always written by the favorite himself with only instructions from the king.[37] In France, as mentioned in the preceding chapter, Cardinal Richelieu was exerting the same kind of "absolute authority" as Olivares in Spain. They were both determined to transform the world. Both men saw it as their personal obligation to improve the long-standing disorders of the state, and both attempted to raise their monarchies and their monarchs to new heights of authority and respect. They were both influenced by the growing seventeenth-century conviction that if man made full use of his powers of reason, he could then exercise some control over events.[38]

It is important to view some of the documents coming from the Junta de Reformación during the Olivares administration, which were offered as proposals for the reform of both the economy and public morality. The pragmatic sanctions of the Junta were published in twenty-three articles concerning the reformation of manners and morals on 10 February,

1623;[39] many of them, as has been noted, repeated Pérez de Herrera's *catorce proposiciones.* These articles of reform were part of the package of Olivares's long-term plan for the remedy, reformation and restoration of Spain. Olivares was seeking to revive the social and political order established by Ferdinand and Isabella and upheld by Philip II.

Briefly, let us look at some of the suggestions of the Junta. The echoes of Pérez de Herrera are everywhere present. To combat the problem of depopulation caused by the great plague of 1596–1602, the Junta attempted to increase the number of marriages in Spain. Those still unwed by the age of twenty-five were to be penalized, brothels were to be abolished, and there was to be a restriction placed on the amount of money permitted for any woman's dowry regardless of her social condition.[40] A further effort to increase and improve the quality of population is embodied in Article XXI, which recommends that Catholic foreigners be permitted to enter the republic, in the hope that they would prosper and increase economic productivity, thus helping to improve the decaying conditions in Spain and making it a more favorable place in which to live.[41]

The Junta de Reformación was also concerned about the problem of unproductive citizens populating the Court. Vagrants who lacked a job that would be advantageous to the Republic and who were the cause of increased crime were to be expelled.[42] The poor were encouraged to work with their hands, or even with their feet, if necessary;[43] the legitimate poor were also to be offered housing and given the opportunity to help the nation with its reform program,[44] and the Junta, like Pérez de Herrera, also proposed that the legitimate poor wear a tattoo on the ears or the hands in order to be identified.[45]

Another concern of the Junta was the excessive sums of money spent for pure ostentation. The Junta proposed that the nobles leave the Court and return to their country estates, in order to prevent them from continuing to spend their money so imprudently. The precious metals, silver and gold, were also forbidden to be utilized as embellishments except for religious, chivalric and battle articles.[46] The Junta also sought to abolish the elaborate and often embellished ruff called the *lechugilla,* which was considered an essential article of a gentleman's wardrobe. Article XIV of the published reform measures insisted that an unadorned piece of fabric cover the collar which, according to the Junta, also had to be considerably reduced in size. The new collar was referred to as the *golilla*.[47] Ultimately this was the only reform measure which took effect.

The Junta also outlawed the large quantities of gold and silver used in metal working,[48]placed restrictions on the possession of foreign tapestries,[49]and recommended a reduction of the amount of money spent on maids, jewelry, home furnishings and clothing.[50]

A major affliction of the Crown's treasury was the excessive amount of silver and gold leaving the nation. Too much money was going out of Spain, and she had to learn to conserve and to utilize the goods produced within her own boundaries.[51] For example, silk factories in Spain were disappearing,[52]and woolen goods once manufactured in La Mancha were being imported from England.[53] Article XII prohibited the selling or purchasing of all cloth, silk or wool, without legal permission. Also Article XIII specifically disallowed the importation of many other items, such as linen, leather, brass, ivory and shell.[54]

Another major proposal of the Junta, which clearly echoes the work of Pérez de Herrera, was for a complete change in the forms of taxation that had been plaguing the people of Spain for years. The aim of the Junta was the abolishment of the *millones*, which were taxes on basic domestic goods. Tax money should also be utilized to give soldiers better salaries in the hope that greater financial rewards would attract more and better soldiers, thus improving the national defense.[55]

Other Junta recommendations included, in Article I, the reduction of the number of government officials by two-thirds in order to cut down on the cost of government,[56] in Article XVIII, the prohibition of the award of important and influential offices through marriage,[57] and in Article VII, the regulation of the number of favors or *mercedes*, as they were called, granted by the king.[58]

The reform program which Olivares sought endlessly to impose turned out to be a failure. The Count-Duke's plea for reform was, as Elliott states, "no more than a monument to his good intentions, the last testament of a frustrated reformer."[59] He was able to diagnose correctly some of the central ills afflicting Castile and the Spanish Monarchy, and proposed a number of antidotes which, if better administered or applied, might have had more beneficial results. Olivares, however, died a frustrated reformer since "the body politic and the body social proved unready to receive them."[60]

NOTES

[1] Elliott, *The Count-Duke*, pp. 87–88. The following survey of Spain's economic problems is drawn from Elliott's work.

[2] Elliott, *The Count-Duke*, pp. 85–87.

[3] Elliott, *The Count-Duke*, p. 87.

[4] Elliott, *The Count-Duke*, p. 48.

[5] Elliott, *The Count-Duke*, p. 56.

[6] Elliott, *The Count-Duke*, pp. 57–58.

[7] Elliott, *The Count-Duke*, pp. 56–57.

[8] Elliott, *The Count-Duke*, pp. 58–59.

[9] Elliott, *The Count-Duke*, p. 61.

[10] Elliott, *The Count-Duke*, p. 61.

[11] Elliott, *The Count-Duke*, pp. 61–62.

[12] Elliott, *The Count-Duke*, p. 62.

[13] Elliott, *The Count-Duke*, p. 64.

[14] Elliott, *The Count-Duke*, pp. 62–63.

[15] Elliott, *The Count-Duke*, p. 65.

[16] Elliott, *The Count-Duke*, pp. 63 and 65.

[17] Elliott, *The Count-Duke*, p. 69.

[18] Elliott, *The Count-Duke*, pp. 76–77.

[19] Elliott, *The Count-Duke*, pp. 71; 75–76.

[20] Elliott, *The Count-Duke*, pp. 69–71.

[21] Cristóbal Espejo, "Enumeración y atribuciones de algunas juntas de la administración española desde el siglo XVI hasta el año 1800," *Revista de la Biblioteca, Archivo y Museo*, año VIII, 32 (1931), p. 342 and p. 356. According to Espejo there was also a special junta established in 1620; see also Angel González Palencia, *La Junta de Reformación* (Valladolid: "Poncelix," 1932), p. 569. González Palencia, in the "Indice de Documentos" included in this book on the 1623 Junta de Reformación also pays attention to all the juntas that had met to discuss a variety of reform concerns beginning as early as 1618; see also Elliott, *The Count-Duke*, p. 104. According to Elliott, the Junta of 1623 was certainly not the first of such attempts at reform; the creation of committees or juntas of ministers for special purposes had become a common practice under Philip III.

[22] Cristóbal Pérez de Herrera. "Proposiciones," in *Proverbios morales L'Espagne du Siècle d'Or* (Madrid: Luis Sánchez, 1618), pp. unnumbered.

[23] Michel Cavillac, "Introducción" to his edition of *Amparo de pobres* by Cristóbal Pérez de Herrera (Madrid: Espasa-Calpe, S.A., 1975), p. xx.

[24] Cavillac, "Introducción," p. lxxvii.

[25] Cavillac, "Introducción," p. clxxii.

[26] Michel Cavillac, *Gueux et Marchands dans le "Guzmán de Alfarache."* (Bordeaux: Institut d Études Ibériques et Ibéro-Americaines de L'Université de Bordeaux, 1983), p. 448.

[27] Cavillac, "Introducción" to *Amparo*, p. xc.

[28] Cavillac, "Introducción" to *Amparo*, pp. xc–xci.

[29] Juan Luis Vives, *Obras—Del socorro de los pobres*. vol. 1, trans. Lorenzo Riber (Madrid: M. Aguilar, 1947), pp. 1368 and 1393–1395.

[30] Vives, p. 1396.

[31] Cavillac, "Introducción" to *Amparo*, pp. xcii–xcvii; see also Pérez de Herrera, *Amparo*, pp. 20–47.

[32] Pérez de Herrera, *Amparo*, pp. 52–64, 122–132, 167.

[33] Pérez de Herrera, *Amparo*, p. 55.

[34] Pérez de Herrera, *Amparo*, pp. 212–213.

[35] Pérez de Herrera, *Amparo*, pp. 269–293.

[36] Elliott, *The Count-Duke*, p. 104.

[37] Elliott, *The Count-Duke*, pp. 296–297.

[38] Elliott, *Richelieu and Olivares* (New York: Cambridge UP, 1984), pp. 166–171.

[39] González Palencia, p. 417.

[40] González Palencia, pp. 443, 391–392, 453–454, 188, 440–442, 258; see also Elliott, *The Count-Duke*, p. 117.

[41] González Palencia, pp. 451–452.

[42] González Palencia, pp. 77–87.

[43] González Palencia, p. 243.

[44] González Palencia, pp. 227–263.

[45] González Palencia, p. 243.

[46] González Palencia, pp. 428–429.

[47] González Palencia, pp. 433–434 and 97–99.

[48] González Palencia, pp. 386–387.

[49] González Palencia, pp. 387 and 429–430.

[50] González Palencia, pp. 390 and 428; see also Elliott, *The Count-Duke*, p.116.

[51] González Palencia, pp. 73–76, 117–129, 167–178, 223–224.

[52] González Palencia, pp. 169–177.

[53] González Palencia, p. 175.

[54] González Palencia, pp. 432–433.

[55] González Palencia, pp. 404–405; see also Elliott, *The Count-Duke*, pp. 122–123.

[56] González Palencia, p. 417.

[57] González Palencia, p. 442.

[58] González Palencia, pp. 38–44, 384–385, 417–422; see also Elliott, *The Count-Duke*, p. 116.

[59] Elliott, *The Count-Duke*, p. 516.

[60] Elliott, *The Count-Duke*, p. 684.

Chapter IV
Political Views in Selected Plays of Lope, Tirso, and Quevedo

With this background in political theory, as well as practice, and Spanish socio-economic distress behind us, we may now look at how the drama of the period sets before its audiences the realities of the world in which they lived. For the theater in Spain, much more than in France or even England, dealt with contemporary events and issues. How truthful it was in its representation of them is a matter of debate. Was it almost universally an apology for the existing system, or did it with some frequency lay open serious flaws in that system? I shall look briefly at the work of three dramatists who are contemporaries of Alarcón before turning to Alarcón, whose theater contains a higher proportion of political and social commentary than that of any of these contemporaries. First though, a look at what the critics say.

A. Critical Judgments about Political Theater of the Day

Many critics, especially those working within the Marxist tradition of social analysis, judge that the theater, because of its popularity among all classes of people, from the royal family and nobility to that of the peasant class, was used as a medium for propaganda. The widespread interest in the theater made it a tool for easy access to the minds and hearts of the Spanish populace. It was a literary creation, as Maravall says, which "nace y se desarrolla con muy definidas finalidades sociales."[1]

José María Díez Borque in his *Sociología de la comedia española del siglo XVII* affirms that the theater written during the first part of Philip IV's reign does not give us an accurate picture of the political, social or economic state of Spain. It was written to disguise the sad truth of the decline of the nation, [2] and the theater became "una total falacia con respecto a la realidad."[3] The theater functioned as a tool of political, social and economic propaganda. For example, in spite of the nation's economic exhaustion, the Court is portrayed in the theater as a haven filled with splendor and luxury.

José Antonio Maravall's *Teatro y literatura en la sociedad barroca*, states the same premise, namely, that the theater was written to defend and strengthen the interests of the monarchy because that monarchy supported the privileges of the nobility and maintained order.[4] The theater, paintings and politics were, as Maravall says, all conditioned by these objectives of propaganda,[5] meant to impose and maintain the pressure of the system of power upon the "pueblo."[6] The theater was used as a political and social instrument.[7] The incorporation, for example, of the countryman and the farmer in the theater was to gain the support of all classes in defense of the monarchical, ministerial and noble levels. The peasant was utilized in plays in order to awaken an interest in, and give a new and positive meaning to, rural living, since many peasants were leaving their unprofitable farm lives to seek a new beginning in the cities. This massive exodus from the farm lands not only caused a visible failure in the agricultural needs of the country, but was also responsible for overcrowding and vast unemployment. Peasants were flattered by having an innate nobility assigned to them in many seventeenth-century plays because of their pure blood (*limpieza de sangre*). The peasant is, as Díez Borque refers to him, "el reducto incontaminado de la limpieza de sangre y la honradez por antonomasia."[8] In other words, the peasant is at the peak of honor since he was assumed not to be tainted with Jewish or Arab blood. Maravall suspects, however, that the development of the rural theme in the theater was due more to the desire to express support for monarchical society than to motives of concern about the faltering agrarian society: the theater directs its energy toward social and political rather than economic concerns.[9]

The propaganda extolling the values and virtues of the monarchical, ministerial and noble society which the theater was intent upon expressing was to manifest to all classes that it was not only the aristocrats who were able to receive acknowledgement and favors, but that anyone, of any class, could also ascend to the highest level of dignity. Thus, undistinguished peasants were portrayed in the theater as possessing virtue and noble values.[10] Another example of how the characters in plays were utilized in order to support the monarchical ideal is the *labrador rico* or wealthy farmer. The nation financially needed him on its side, and the theater was again manipulated for propaganda purposes. He was needed to support the royal treasury, and to help to reestablish the agrarian economy. In short, the wealthy farmer represented a strong force, both economic and social, whose support was needed in defense and conservation of social order. The appearance of this wealthy farmer in the theater suspiciously coincided with the economic and social crisis of the 1600's. In the plays, he appears as a rich and virtuous man, respectful of social order. One of the objectives of the Baroque theater was to offer these *labradores* a kind of public compensation for the loyalty they had shown to their nation, or as a way to persuade them to defend the established order if they were not inclined to do so. In the theater, therefore, this wealthy farmer, who was a strong social and economic influence, is portrayed as a rich and virtuous man who lives a happy life because of the respect he gives to social order. He and his children are seen as ascending the social ladder and are even married into the noble class by none other than the king himself.[11]

The theme of honor also plays an important role in the Spanish theater. This theme acts as another elevated form of propaganda just as the theme of obedience to the king does. Maravall sees honor as yet another tool of propaganda in the Baroque theater which serves the interests of the monarchical form of government.

The theater of the seventeenth century is generally marked, say Díez-Borque and Maravall among others, by a very conservative tone which can be explained in part by the fact that playwrights, working to get ahead, often received acclaim and a government post because they produced panegyrics designed to please the heads of state. It was advantageous for playwrights to portray a favorable image of the king and his minister in their work, since political favors were often granted to those writers who could please the royal ministers and king by singing their praises in the popular genre of the drama. One can only imagine the competitive, envious and cut-throat business that drama became. Playwrights, fighting for their fame, would have to scratch and claw their way up the ladder of success, criticizing whoever presented himself as a threat to their success. As Ruth Lee Kennedy has pointed out, there was much competition among promising dramatists between the years 1616 and 1621. "The greatest talents of Spain were being drawn to Madrid as though by a magnet, some of them after long years abroad."[12] Therefore, it was not only a time of political, social and economic decay but also a time of literary war.

Leicester Bradner, not a Marxist critic, basically joins with the Marxists, though for different reasons, in denying the serious political concerns of the seventeenth-century dramatists. He says that the Spanish dramatists usually exploited the personal and emotional aspects in their work. They preferred, he says, to stress feelings of admiration for particular individuals or feelings of sympathy for their failures, rather than to center their attention on the "issues of good and bad government."[13] Spanish dramatists therefore preferred "to attempt to arouse sympathy" of their spectators for the fallen *privado* and to stress "the inevitable turning of fortune's wheel."[14] They also preferred to highlight the personal relationships of the characters, making them the center of dramatic interest,[15] rather than to overstep their grounds and to perhaps fall out of favor by dealing with more dangerous political topics.

Unlike critics Díez Borque, Maravall, and Bradner, Kennedy maintains that there is a good deal of political concern demonstrated in seventeenth-century plays. She has pointed out that the years 1617 to 1625 were extremely important years for Spanish literature in which writers really permeated their work with suggestions about how to help the suffering nation. "They were years in which the agitation for change threw into clear, sharp relief the political decay, the economic disorder, and the social corruption that were rotting the national fabric...For us it is particularly important that they were years that to many seemed to cry aloud for a more serious theater than was offered by the Lopean formula of love, honor, and intrigue—one that should perform the corrective function that had, at least in theory, been allotted that genre since the days of Aristotle and Horace."[16]

B. Alarcón's Contemporaries

1. The Theater of Lope de Vega
In the theater of Lope de Vega it is easy to find confirmation of Maravall's and Díez Borque's views. The "innate conservativism" of his plays, as Díez Borque refers to it, serves to reinforce the acceptance of the king as the incarnation of the power of God here on earth. Obedience and loyalty to the king therefore become a kind of religious responsibility on the part of all subjects.[17] The religious connotation attached to obedience to the king is especially notable in plays written during the period of Philip IV.[18]

Although I will not deal at any length with Lope de Vega in this study, it can be stated generally that Lope's dramas are usually conservative and conformist in nature, focusing attention mainly on love, honor and intrigue.[19] The theater of Lope de Vega (1562–1635) faithfully portrays the figure of the absolute monarch with dignity and reverence.[20] Even in dramas like *El villano en su rincón* which criticizes the frivolity of court life, or such a play as the magnificent *Fuenteovejuna*, with its dangerous attack on corrupt nobility, the figures of the monarchs (the Catholic Sovereigns Ferdinand and Isabel), are portrayed with maximum reverence. Obedience to the king's wishes is held in the highest regard because it is the support and foundation of absolutism. Lope attempts, as Maravall states, to introduce "al pueblo en la escena, haciéndole participar, en cierto modo y medida, en los valores de la capa superior y atrayéndole por ese camino a la defensa de los mismos."[21] Lope highlights Philip IV as the Spanish king who is the model of perfection, and attributes all errors in government matters to his subjects.[22] He had, after all, stated in a private letter that: "El sello del govierno es santo, no hay tan mala yuntençion [*sic*] que no lo confiesse; pero nuestros pecados desazen cuantos consejos toman."[23]

Díez Borque also traces through various plays of Lope the glorification of the figure of Philip IV. *La juventud de San Isidro*, which Professors Morley and Bruerton have dated 1622,[24] clearly portrays a favorable image of Philip IV's military accomplishments while avoiding mention of defeats.[25] Lope also applauds Spanish defense of the Indies in *El Brasil restituido* [26] (1625) [27] as another way of praising the efforts of Philip IV. *La noche de San Juan* (1631) [28] is yet another example of glorification and praise for Philip IV even in the face of total disaster for Spain during these critical years, when everything seemed to be falling apart: the *vellón* coin was rapidly devaluating; the loss of the Spanish naval fleet at Matanzas (1628) was of great significance; the Dutch were taking the offensive against Spain, the economy of the nation was continuing to decline as the influx of silver from the Indies dropped, and the relationship between France and Spain was becoming more strained.[29]

Love, fear and obedience are the three *vínculos* that join the subject to his king. These are the three key concepts which Lope's theater insists upon,[30] while largely shunning expressions of political criticism and concern.

2. The Theater of Tirso de Molina

Tirso de Molina (1584–1648) is known as one of the most vigorous defenders of Lope's dramatic formula against Neo-Aristotelian critics. Yet, a number of his plays are far from uncritical about society and government and implicitly disapproving of the government of Philip IV. It should be remembered that Tirso, like so many ecclesiastics, always felt specially privileged to attack temporal powers.

Tirso had been an admirer of Philip III, whom he viewed, no doubt wrongly, as a "wise and deeply religious ruler, one outstanding for his gentleness and for the purity of his personal life. He was a leader whose spiritual qualities had brought to his people God's richest blessings, making the Spain of his time a veritable promised land of milk and honey, delivering it from the afflictions of famine, disease, war, the harsh inclemencies of Heaven, and making it possible for the nation to enjoy, without opposition or fear, her wealth, her peace, and her religion."[31] Tirso warmly praises Philip III and the Archbishop Sandoval y Rojas, whose nephew was none other than the Duke of Lerma. Perhaps he did not wish to criticize either Lerma or his son Uceda for fear that such criticism would in turn hurt the two men he admired most, the king and the archbishop.[32] When the new, young Philip took over the throne in 1621 after his father's death, Tirso grew bitter toward Philip IV and his minister, Olivares. Kennedy states that Tirso later in revenge "refashioned" many of his plays in order to express his bitterness against Olivares. He was, as Kennedy says, "a very "communicative dramatist," one who "drew heavily from the milieu that surrounded him, particularly during his Madrid period."[33] His hatred toward the new regime kept increasing, insists Kennedy, so that as early as 1622, Tirso can be described as "bitterly critical" of Olivares and his administration.[34] In 1625, he was banished from the Court by Olivares's Junta de Reformación and enjoined to write no more plays.

Kennedy mentions four plays which she considers to be politically dangerous works. They are such powerful works as *La prudencia en la mujer*, *Privar contra su gusto*, *La mujer que manda en casa*, and the *auto sacramental*, *Los hermanos parecidos*, all of which, she says, illustrate Tirso's favor of the old regime and his opposition toward the new one under Olivares.[35] Tirso, as we have said, was a dramatist who drew inspiration from the happenings of his own time; but he was well read in

Spanish history and drew information from his contemporary Juan de Mariana's *Historia general de España*. All of these plays, according to Kennedy, make evident Tirso's "profound interest in the political situation of Spain."[36]

In this study the plots of two of these plays will be examined to illustrate the satire that Tirso was perhaps aiming at Olivares and his court officials, since they deal with the relationship between the king and his *privado* and the evil such powerful men may do. It is, however, equally likely that, because these plays were written when the Olivares regime had only just begun, Tirso was merely satirizing the defects of government at its top levels and drawing attention to certain contemporary issues in general without actually blaming anyone in particular.

La prudencia en la mujer was composed, according to Kennedy, in 1622.[37] Tirso intended to satirize poor methods of government in this play, and he cleverly utilized material from Mariana's *Historia general de España* to achieve this goal. The Queen of the play, Doña María de Molina, is really the historical María Alfonso de Meneses, relative of Alfonso el Sabio, who, after the death of her husband, served as Queen Regent during the minority of her son Fernando (1295–1301). Tirso used the *Chronicle of Fernando IV* for this bit of historical information, but he generally uses Juan de Mariana as his historical source in this play. The episode which Blanca de los Ríos calls "La cena de la Reina"[38] takes place in scene 17 of the second act. Blanca de los Ríos suggests that Tirso, a great enthusiast of Queen Isabel de Borbón, wife of Philip IV, used this episode to throw darts at Olivares, whose relations with the young queen were never very good. Mariana's account states, according to Blanca de los Ríos, that the Queen, during the reign of Henry III (1390–1406), was deprived of a meal on various occasions, while the wealthy grandees stuffed themselves and wasted food freely.[39] Tirso also takes information from Mariana concerning the reign of Henry III, during which corrupt officials usurped the royal power of the king.[40]

This historical play revolves around the struggle of the scheming Infantes don Enrique, don Juan, and don Diego de Haro and the widowed Queen, doña María de Molina, whose husband, King Sancho IV, has valiantly died in battle. The ambitious Infantes each attempts to devise a plan by which to gain control of the government by marrying the Queen. Their endeavors are frustrated by this prudent and courageous Queen, who can see straight through their self-interested tactics. She is portrayed

as a strong woman, left alone to raise a young king, "que apenas hablar
sabe,"[41] able to attend to government affairs, and capable of dealing with
the vulture-like Infantes. The Queen, whose intelligence is not surpassed
by her ministers', is clearly aware of their perverse intentions. She wants
no part of a marriage to any of these avaricious men:

> Ya yo sé que no el amor,
> sino la codicia avara
> del reino que pretendéis,
> os da bárbara esperanza
> de que he de ser vuestra esposa;...

and goes on to attack the invasion of the debased currency *vellón*, a
problem clearly not of the thirteenth century but the seventeenth. (pp.
906–907).

She insists that her son is the rightful heir to the throne. The young
king, still a child however, is disheartened by all the contention at Court,
so the Queen returns with him to her home town of León. The child king
expresses his negative sentiments about the wily ministers when he tells
his mother that he will cut their heads off himself, "Cortaréles la cabeza,
/ por vida de mi padre" (p. 909).

The Infante and royal *privado* don Juan is so corrupt in his attempt to
gain control of the Crown that he takes advantage of the Queen's absence
to try to convince everyone that the young king is the fruit of an incestu-
ous union. He recommends that both the Queen and her son be placed in
prison, thus giving him royal power. No action is too vile in the eyes of a
courtier whose aim is absolute power (not only in the fourteenth century
but at the Court of Philip IV). The Infante Enrique boldly protests that
an unarmed woman and child cannot stand in the way of his success:

> Ni una mujer desarmada
> es bien que temor nos dé
> con un niño. (p. 916)

The remainder of Act I reveals even more horrifying aspects of these
plotting ministers, whose malicious, self-interested actions multiply as
the play develops. They also conspire to feign their loyalty to the Queen
in an attempt to gain control through deceptive measures.

In Act II, the perverse Infante don Juan seeks the unscrupulous aid of
the Jewish court doctor, Ismael, who schemes to win control for his
sponsor by poisoning the child king. Unmindful of Bodinian theory

about the divinity of the king, the Infante has become consumed by the desire for power. Ismael feels no remorse, since his law permits the killing of a Christian, and the benefits that he will receive are deliciously enticing. However, when confronted by the Queen, Ismael admits to his guilt, confessing that he agreed to the poisoning for fear of don Juan's punishment. We are left with a feeling of total indignation. There is no loyalty even among the evil conspirators themselves. The target of criticism was perhaps the lack of ethics common in everyday court life where self-interest and back-stabbing flourished. The Queen, on the other hand, is portrayed as the essence of virtue and stands out in contrast to the vice of the people at Court. She, in conformity with Bodin, views the young king as an "ángel de Dios" (p. 922). Intent upon ridding the nation of all the traitors, she commands Ismael either to drink the poison that he prepared for the child king or be dragged naked through the streets. He chooses the deadly potion in order to avoid public shame and reveals his conversion to Christianity by not questioning the propriety of his sentence: "Quien contra su rey se atreve, / es digno de aqueste pago"(p. 922). He drinks the poison and dramatically calls out to the Messiah upon his death!

Later, the Queen openly discusses with don Juan the treason she suspects is being plotted against her and her son. He tries to draw suspicion away from himself by stating that he too feels that he is a victim of treason and has been set up to take the blame.

In scene 10 of Act II, don Juan discovers the body of Ismael and is now aware of how the Queen acquired her information. He desperately attempts suicide, the ultimate sin in Christian terms, with a poisonous solution, but the Queen's presence interrupts his sacrilegious action. She proceeds to ask him bluntly: "¿Vos sois noble?, ¿vos cristiano? / Don Juan, ¿vos teméis a Dios?" (p. 927). The Queen, a Christian and God-fearing woman, is appalled at the thought that don Juan would attempt to take his own life. She tells him that she does not hold him in less esteem than she did before, since she had learned of his intended treason from "un hebreo vil" whose testimony she does not consider valid. She warns him, however, against his excessive ambitions, saying that since the staff of justice, held high, observes all errors and crimes, he cannot expect to evade detection in crime:

> El papel que os escribí,
> es para daros noticia

> de que en cualquier yerro o falta
> ve mucho, por ser tan alta,
> la vara de la justicia;... (p. 928)

Don Juan then commits his worst act of treachery when he spreads the word that the Queen herself had tried to poison her son because of her own ambition. He explains her apparent goodness to be "una santidad fingida" (p. 930). The other ministers, however, have learned to love and respect the Queen and do not believe don Juan's story.

The Queen is forced to imprison don Juan when he blatantly admits to having plotted the murder of the child king in order to satisfy his appetite for power. He accepts his sentence as just when he says:

> Quien a ser traidor se inclina,
> tarde volverá en su acuerdo.
> La libertad y honra pierdo
> por mi ambicioso interés:
> callar y sufrir, pues es
> por la pena el loco, cuerdo. (p. 934)

As spokesman for Tirso, the Queen offers a description of the manner in which a king should rule a nation in the first scene of Act III. The young King is now seventeen years old, approximately the same age as Philip IV was when he assumed the throne, although her advice could very well refer to Philip III and Lerma's relationship. She first tells her son that the only true reason of state that exists is service to God: "porque no hay razón de estado / como es el servir a Dios" (p. 936). She warns him not to hand the reins of power over to the *privado* forgetting that the government of the nation is solely his duty as the king.

> Nunca os dejéis gobernar
> de privados, de manera
> que salgáis de vuestra esfera,
> ni les lleguéis tanto a dar
> que se arrojen de tal modo
> al cebo del interés,
> que os fuercen, hijo, después
> a que se lo quitéis todo. (p. 936)

In order to avoid envy at Court and to maintain the necessary respect of his vassals, he must never shower favors on any one particular person. Instead she tells him to be equally generous to all:

> Con todos los grandes sed
> tan igual y generoso,
> que nadie quede quejoso
> de que a otro hacéis más merced:
> tan apacible y discreto,
> que a todos seáis amable;
> mas [*sic*] no tan comunicable
> que os pierdan, hijo, el respeto. (p. 936)

The young King is also reminded of the importance of public audiences in order to maintain the esteem of his vassals. These audiences, she says, will prove that he respects his people as they in turn must respect him:

> Alegrad vuestros vasallos,
> saliendo en público a vellos;
> que no os estimarán ellos,
> si no os preciáis de estimallos.
> Cobraréis de amable fama
> con quien vuestra vista goce;
> que lo que no se conoce,
> aunque se teme, no se ama. (p. 936)

The king should also not be influenced by flattery but allow it only to entertain him:

> De juglares lisonjeros,
> si no podéis excusaros,
> no uséis para aconsejaros,
> sino para entreteneros. (p. 936)

The military should love and honor their king, since it is love and not the sword that conquers. Soldiers who revere their sovereign will naturally fight harder than those who do not:

> Sea por vos estimada
> la milicia en vuestra tierra,
> porque más vence en la guerra
> el amor que no la espada. (p. 936)

She also encourages her son to allow doctors and men of nobility to enter into the nation in order to help Spain back to her feet. These men, however, should be of the same faith, "que suele la cristianidad / alcanzar más que la ciencia" (p. 937). Her words were perhaps intended to criticize proposals suggested by Pérez de Herrera and Olivares to bring Portuguese Jews back into Spain in order to cure its financial troubles.

Lastly she tells him to reign with prudence and at all times to remember his value as the king of Spain. As they both prepare to leave one another, the Queen offers her son one more bit of advice concerning his presence at the "cortes de Madrid," which she feels to be indispensable: "Asistid / a las cortes de Madrid; / que es de importancia que esté / en ellas vuestra presencia;..." (p. 937).

Don Juan, after ten years of imprisonment for treason, continues his perverse behavior and conspires with don Enrique, don Alvaro and don Nuño to win the favor of the King with their deception and lies. Don Enrique tells the King that it was the two Caravajal brothers who were the ones who attempted to usurp royal power while the others agree and offer their assistance against the Caravajal family. The King is convinced of the family's guilt, and plans to imprison the brothers.

The conspiracy of the four evil ministers involves the Queen, who is ordered imprisoned by the King himself. He is convinced by these ministers that his own mother was planning to take control of the government. At this moment of shock for the Queen, don Juan plays on her panic, offering his hand in marriage in order to save her from imprisonment. The totally evil character of don Juan is again emphasized as he attempts to play both sides of the fence by saying that with their union they can then be rid of a king whom he accuses of being "tan inhumano" (p. 948). He pretends that the four evil ministers have, all along, been on her side. She, of course, does not fall into the trap and flatly refuses the offer. Unlike her son, an inexperienced, young king, she is able to see through the lies of the scheming minister.

Disregarding the advice of don Juan, the King finally meets with his mother, who begins to unravel the entire truth to her son. The stories of the scheming ministers, she says, are a pack of lies and don Juan, through the workings of an evil Jew, had attempted to murder him when he was a child. She produces the letter which don Juan had given her asking for her hand in marriage, and in which he suggests joining the forces of don Enrique and don Nuño against him.

Three of the evil ministers, fearful of their fate, flee to Aragón. The King asks his mother to suggest the proper punishment for don Juan, whom they still have in custody. Her suggestion is to banish him from the kingdom, confiscating his estates and his belongings, and to award them to the Caravajal brothers and to the loyal don Juan Benavides, who have never been traitors. The King praises the valor and prudence of his mother, and with the promise of a continuation, the play ends.

It is clear that *La prudencia en la mujer* is a serious play about the problems of government. It is also clearly in the camp of anti-*privado* theorists, much unlike Quevedo as we see him in his play *Cómo ha de ser el privado*. Perhaps, as Kennedy suggests, it is an attack on the Olivares administration; perhaps the character of don Juan, portrayed as a ruthless and overly ambitious minister, satirizes the figure of the powerful Olivares. It is also possible that the young and inexperienced king, so easily persuaded by the four evil ministers, was meant to be a cautionary drawing of Philip IV, who coincidentally took the throne at approximately the same age as the king in the play. All this is possible, but we should keep in mind that the date given this play (1622) is only one year after the Olivares faction attained power. Could Tirso have come to hate Olivares that much in such a short period of time? It seems more likely that Tirso intended only to warn young Philip IV of the disasters that can befall a nation when an unsuspecting king is manipulated by ambitious, self-interested ministers. Tirso wanted the play to act as a reminder to Philip IV of his kingly responsibilities and to take personal charge of his administration, rather than to hand over the reins of power to some ruthless and aspiring men.

A second play by Tirso, *Privar contra su gusto*, also offers harsh political commentary, so harsh that it may have offended Olivares deeply and thus led to Tirso's banishment from Court after 1625. It may also have been retouched at a later date, as Kennedy suggests, like *La prudencia en la mujer*, as a form of retaliation against Olivares.[42] But whatever the motives behind this play, it describes the life of a dedicated and perfect *privado*, very unlike the *privado* seen in the preceding play.

The action takes place in Naples, perhaps during the rule of Fernando II (1495–1496). Kennedy believes that this play was written or perhaps rewritten between the years 1620–1621,[43] and Blanca de los Ríos dates it between the years 1632–1634.[44] This latter critic is of the opinion that Tirso had intended this work to satirize Quevedo's refusal to accept the high posts that both Olivares and Philip IV offered him.[45] It can also be considered as a satire or "rotunda e indignada respuesta,"[46] according to Blanca de los Ríos, aimed at Quevedo, who had offended Tirso in his "El

Chitón de las taravillas" of 1630, the publication of which won Quevedo the favor of the Crown and Olivares. One may also regard it as in part a satire on the late marriage of Quevedo to a woman from Aragón, whom Tirso has dubbed with the surname "Aragón."[47] Kennedy sees it as a daring work of opposition aimed at the new regime for injuries caused Tirso.[48] So many, and such contradictory, interpretations of the play's message and the uncertainty about its date warn us to proceed with caution in specifying precisely the objects of satire. Whatever else may be hidden in the text, the drama does offer a portrait of an exemplary *privado* in the character of don Juan de Cardona.

This *privado* is the epitome of what a loyal and respectable minister should be. He seeks what is best for his king, don Fadrique of Naples, and for his nation rather than what would most benefit him. As in the case of *La prudencia en la mujer*, the date of this play, according to Kennedy (1620–1621), closely coincides with the date of Philip IV's accession to the throne and the inception of the Olivares regime. It therefore seems possible that Tirso intended this play to be a source of inspiration for Olivares, as well, perhaps, of warning to the young Philip IV, whose amorous dalliances were well known.

In Act I, we see King Fadrique on a hunting trip in the countryside when he sights the beautiful Leonora, sister of don Juan de Cardona. Devoid of self-control and filled with lustful desires toward her, he openly proclaims his affections for her. She, however, a woman of honor, rudely responds to her admirer, unaware at this moment that her suitor is, in fact, the King himself. Tirso immediately criticizes life at Court in the words of this chaste woman:

> Peligro el campo amenaza,
> todo es engaño en la caza,
> todo en la corte es fingido.
> Si venido
> habéis al campo a cazar
> de la corte, será en vano
> lisonjear,
> pues, cazador cortesano,
> no vendréis sino a engañar.[49]

The suitor later identifies himself as the king, and Leonora then behaves respectfully toward him, but she is still vigilant of her honor. She complains that his father, the late king, once employed a *privado* who eventually fell from power. She identifies this *privado* as her father:

> Con vuestro padre privó
> el nuestro en tiempos pasados,
> y paró en lo que privados
> suelen: volaba, y cayó. (p. 1077)

Her brother, now of modest fortune, has been able to offer her great security and freedom away from the envy that necessarily accompanies wealth and power.

Before leaving the King's presence, Leonora again proves her honorable character by saying that his power as king has no effect on her as a woman: "que el poder / en el campo, y con amor, / no asegura a una mujer" (p. 1077). The sacredness of her honor is contrasted with the concupiscence of the King who, still driven by lustful passion, is intent upon gaining her affections.

In scene 5 of the first act, masked men attempt the assassination of the King. Luckily for him, Leonora's brother, don Juan, and another loyal vassal, don Luis, are there to defend his life. The unknown men escape the swords of don Juan and don Luis. The King is appreciative of don Juan for saving his life and wishes to reward him magnificently with honors and monetary favors: "…yo premiaré / tu socorro y tu lealtad / tanto, que a la eternidad / altares y estatuas dé." "Y en mi agradecimiento / obligaciones, que pagar intento" (p. 1080).

In scene 8 of this first act, don Juan takes the opportunity to tell the King that the enormous strain of the government post on his father was far too burdensome for him to bear; therefore, he fled the Court, filled with flattery and favors, to a more serene life in the country:

> .... Cansado
> del intolerable peso
> del reino, carga cruel,
> que de sus hombros fió
> el rey Alfonso, paró
> en dar en tierra con él.
> Obligaron desengaños
> a que huyendo aduladores
> y desmintiendo favores,
> diese quietud a sus años
> y lición al escarmiento
> en aquesta soledad,

> cuya quieta amenidad
> nos dejó por testamento;...(p. 1081)

Fadrique says that perhaps his father, the late king Alfonso, was unjust to this minister since far too much was expected of him:

> Mi padre, mal informado,
> dió a don Pedro pago injusto,
> pudiendo más que su gusto
> ciegas razones de Estado. (p. 1081)

The King wishes to make don Juan his *privado* since he feels indebted to him for having saved his life. He suspects that don Luis de
Moncada may have been one of the masked men and considers him dangerous. Don Juan, however, is able to convince the King of don Luis's
innocence by reporting that he aided him in saving his life.

In scene 12, when the King requests that don Juan become his royal
privado, Don Juan hesitates, describing his father's past experiences and
stating that he would prefer to follow his father's advice by remaining far
from the vices at Court. He says that his prudent father rejected riches,
titles and possessions, preferring "...consejos prudentes, / antídotos del
peligro, / remedio contra ambiciones, / y contrayerba de vicios" (p.
1086). Don Juan continues this long harangue against court life in this
way:

> Todos éstos se cifraron
> en el provechoso olvido
> del palacio y de la corte
> de quien mil veces nos dijo
> tanto mal, tantos engaños,
> ceremonias, artificios,
> dobleces, contradicciones,
> envidias, falsos amigos,
> que connaturalizó
> en nosotros desde niños
> su sabio aborrecimiento; (p. 1086)

All of these complaints coming from don Juan perhaps illustrate
Tirso's own political point of view. Tirso, however, elects the perfect
privado to be the spokesman against the corrupt society at Court.

The King resorts to flattery in order to convince don Juan to accept
the offered position. He states just how lucky he is to have a good and

wise friend such as don Juan by his side. Don Juan, however, who has been counselled by his father, is wise enough to see through the King and protests, saying that he prefers truth over flattery: "Señor, / más ha de poder conmigo / la verdad, que la lisonja" (p. 1086). Nonetheless, since don Juan is a virtuous man who is always respectful of the wishes of his King, he reluctantly asssumes his appointed post as *privado.* The King, well aware of the loyalty and nobility of this man, has succeeded in forcing him against his will, thus illustrating the title of the play: "pero por el mismo caso / que a un rey habéis resistido, / habéis de privar por fuerza;..." (p. 1087). Don Juan's response to the King is as follows: "Testigos / sed deste milagro, cielos, / pues contra mi gusto privo" (p. 1088).

In Act II, don Juan, as *privado,* announces Octavio's promotion to "general de las galeras." Octavio is so pleased that he wishes to kiss the hand of the *privado,* whom he considers to have been his intercessor. Don Juan feels offended by Octavio's desire to kiss him. The *privado* should never be indulged in ways befitting only a king, nor should a *privado* be exempt from customary court practices : "no excepcionan la privanza / leyes que el palacio puso" (p. 1088). A *privado* should not take advantage of his position by seeking excessive liberties.

Don Juan's conscientious attitude of responsibility is apparent when he admits to himself that he cannot mix reason of state and love together. His concern for the well-being of the state far exceeds his personal desires for the love of a woman: "pues nunca se llevan bien / razón de estado y amor" (p. 1089). Don Juan, in a later scene, repeats this same fear of mixing love and his responsibilities as *privado* when he tells don Luis:

> Condené al fuego su liga, [that of the Infanta Isabella]
> y aunque injusto en tal venganza,
> mi ocupación ha podido
> sanar mi amor con su olvido;
> que esto debo a mi privanza. (pp. 1091–1092);
> [emphasis added]

Leonora again acts as a vehicle for Tirso's criticism of the dangers of court life. She expresses her concern for her brother, who she feels is caught in a tempest at sea:

> soy yo vuestra hermana, y temo
> las violencias del poder.

> Ponderad cuál es mayor,
> el mío o vuestro temor:
> vos en el mar proceloso
> del gobierno peligroso,
> yo en los riesgos de mi honor. (p. 1090)

Don Juan becomes suspicious that the King wants to have him as his *privado* so as to give him access to his sister, Leonora. Don Juan finds himself caught in a real dilemma since he feels torn between his duty to his King and the protection of his own honor. (This situation is very similar to the *privado*'s dilemma in Alarcón's *Los pechos privilegiados*, discussed below.) He articulates his anxiety in this way:

> Buena prueba es el amor
> con que Fadrique pretende
> hacerme por él favor;
> pero caro me le vende,
> si ha de costarme el honor. (p. 1090)

As the play develops, don Juan feels increasingly imprisoned by his position as *privado* and would like to be relieved from it. He voices his feelings of concern to don Luis:

> Don Lüis,[*sic*] mi libertad
> ya se perdió, ya no es mía
> después que en el puesto estoy
> que rehusé por tantos modos,
> todo he de ser para todos,
> y nada para mí soy.
> Mi privanza es un Argel
> donde, en cautiverio largo,
> cadenas de tanto cargo
> me dan tormento crüel.
> Lastimaos de ver que privo,
> forzando mi voluntad,
> y no culpéis amistad
> de preso ni de cautivo,
> si falta a correspondencias
> y no cumple obligaciones. (p. 1091)

Don Juan decides that in order to remedy the precarious situation of his honor, he must marry his sister to a suitor in Aragón. Upon learning of the proposed marriage, however, the King becomes furious. He commands that neither Leonora marry in Aragón, nor don Juan be excused from his post as *privado*: "mas [*sic*] ni Leonora se ha de ir, / ni os habéis vos de eximir / de mi favor y privanza" (p. 1095).

Intermingled with the theme of a forced *privanza* and the tensions that go along with this situation are the love intrigue between Leonora, who loves the King, and the King, who only desires to dishonor her; between don Juan and the Infanta, the King's sister; and between don Luis and Clavela. Don Juan, however, is caught in the middle between Clavela and don Luis, and relationships therefore become strained. He is convinced that a *privado* is unable to have friends: "¡Privar y tener amigos! / Nadie alcanzó dicha tanta" (p. 1098). The spectator, instead of envying the power of don Juan's position, is left with a feeling of pity for him. This sorrowful picture of a friendless *privado* clearly illustrates the difficult position of a royal *valido*. Don Juan is portrayed as a virtuous yet lonely man since he never compromises integrity for the sake of friendship. Through the example of don Juan, it was made clear to all who attended the drama, and especially to the new favorite, Olivares, how lonely his position might be if he were to be a disinterested and honorable minister.

The lustful King continues to scheme to dishonor Leonora. He decides to burden don Juan with an abundance of paperwork to keep him busy and out of the way. He locks his *privado* in the office and waits to see just how much of the task he is able to complete. This method will allow the King to determine whether or not the *privado* has remained in the room diligently working. Don Juan, however, is too clever for the plotting sovereign's ruse. He knows Fadrique well and is also well aware of his passion for his sister. Therefore, he too contrives a plan by which to fool the King.

Meanwhile we learn of Horacio and Rugero's plan to murder Fadrique in order to gain power as *privado*(s) to the heir apparent, the Count of Anjou, who plans to take over Naples:

> Con su muerte aseguremos
> el reino que desea
> el de Anjou, pues al punto que se vea
> a la silla admitido,
> su privanza y favor nos ha ofrecido. (p. 1099)

The astute don Juan, however, is aware of their plans. The spectator soon realizes that the evil Horacio and Rugero have also conspired to aid the King in his lustful desires.

Don Juan is ready and waiting with his own plan to delude the King into thinking that he is in fact a wise stranger who has come with the purpose of guiding the actions of the sovereign along the right path. Don Juan, concealing his face in order to keep his identity unknown, informs the King that he wishes to instruct him concerning the dangers that exist for his life and the future of his government:

> Antes que de aquí me parta,
> tengo, señor, de deciros
> muchas cosas de importancia
> a vuestra vida y gobierno,
> que peligra de ignorarlas. (p. 1101)

The King is dumbfounded at the candidness of the stranger and demands that he identify himself, to which don Juan retorts: "Soy quien penetro vuestra alma, / y sé vuestros pensamientos" (p. 1101). Don Juan is able to rattle the conscience of the King when he asks him to explain his intentions of dishonoring Leonora with false plans of marriage while, at the same time, promising his hand to another woman, the Infanta of Sicilia:

> Viene a fingir que ha de ser
> su esposo para obligarla,
> cuando en Sicilia pretende
> desposarse con su infanta. (p. 1101)

Fadrique is astonished that the remarks coming from the stranger are so accurate. He suspects the stranger to be don Juan since he is the only person who shares such knowledge because of their close contact. The voice of the stranger, however, does not resemble that of don Juan. The King is then told by the unknown person that Horacio and Rugero are conspiring to kill him. The stranger, having locked the two traitors in a room, then gives King Fadrique the key as proof. He further persuades the King to go and see for himself. In return the stranger requests that the King never ask his identity and that he never again come to the window of Leonora at this late hour. The stranger recommends several pieces of advice to the King: if he does not intend to marry Leonora, he should forget her: "...si no es que intentas como a esposa sublimarla, / olvides;..." (p. 1103). He also requests that the sovereign be more moderate and prudent by not awarding so many favors as he has done so generously in the past: "...que reprimas / el curso a mercedes tantas /

como le haces, pues siempre / fué prudente la templanza" (p. 1103). He explains that this liberality of gifts is the cause of much envy at Court: "Aborrecible es a todos / después que tanto le ensalzas, / y ocasionando a la envidia / le expones a mil desgracias" (p. 1103). He also entreats the King to reduce some of the administrative power of his *privado* don Juan, who is not the king and should, therefore, never be given so much power in government matters since: "El privado es inferior / a su rey;..." (p. 1103). Lastly he recommends that the sovereign marry Clavela to don Luis de Moncada since he has been a loyal servant.

The King agrees to oblige these requests since they seem rather simple when compared to the fact that the stranger has probably saved his life and his kingdom from the two conspirators. The King, then, taking the stranger's advice, dashes off to arrest the traitors Horacio and Rugero.

Fadrique remains suspicious that the prudent stranger is his *privado* don Juan. He rushes back to the office where he had left him earlier with a lot of paper work to accomplish. In Act III, the King discovers that don Juan has completed all the letters he had requested him to write. Since it would be impossible for don Juan to have been in two places at the same time, the King is satisfied, believing that the stranger could not possibly have been his royal *privado*.

Don Juan, on the other hand, is elated that his scheme has been successful. He has persuaded the King to leave behind his sensual "amor ciego" and he no longer needs to be concerned about his honor (p. 1104).

Don Juan continues the ruse when the King, following the suggestion of the stranger, proposes that don Luis take over the post of *mayordomo mayor*, thus relieving don Juan of some of his duties. Don Juan pretends to protest, saying that the post has been his for some time; he wonders what wrong he may have done now to be considered unworthy of the position: "...pero ese cargo / que yo hasta agora [*sic*] he ejercido, / si no lo he desmerecido..." (p. 1105). He continues to pretend that he is upset over having lost the post in order to cover up the scheme which he had planned so well.

The King relates the story of the stranger to don Juan and don Luis: just as the stranger had informed him, he found barrels of gun powder in Horacio and Rugero's possession. He then informs don Juan that, as the stranger had advised him, he is going to reduce more of the responsibili-

ties of his *privado* in order to rid the Court of the envy which has become
so prevalent:

> No tiene mucha fe en vos,
> quien quiera que él haya sido,
> pues que me ruega que os quite
> muchos, don Juan, de los cargos,
> que con beneficios largos
> os di, y que no os necesite
> a que tengáis envidiosos. (p. 1106)

Don Juan protests, questioning again what he has done to deserve such
humiliation. Of course, however, his questions are inserted only to keep
the suspicion of the King away from him.

The passion that the King once felt for Leonora has now cooled since
he has taken the advice of the stranger. He tells her that he must give her
hand to another.

Although Fadrique no longer suspects don Juan of the contrivance,
Leonora and don Luis are not so convinced. Both of these characters are
angry with don Juan. Don Luis believes that don Juan has an interest in
the woman he loves, and Leonora feels that don Juan is jealous of the
King's affections for her and is therefore deliberately trying to terminate
their relationship.

Don Juan plans to reappear as the stranger to the King in scene 8 of
this final act. His motive for the scheme this time is to request that the
sovereign wed his sister, Leonora, since he is aware of her deep feelings
for him.

The spectator learns that the King owes a sum of "cien mil ducados"
to the state. He also learns that don Juan plans to depart the following
day just as his father did to escape the evils at Court. He invites Marco
Antonio to appraise his own personal belongings, which he will use to
pay the King's debt. Don Juan's generosity to the Crown is overwhelm-
ing. True virtue, in his opinion, is never self-seeking: "…que la virtud /
nunca interesable ha sido" (p. 1111). Marco is also asked not to divulge
this information to anyone: "Sólo, Marco Antonio, os pido / que secreto
aquesto esté. / No sepa este desempeño, / ni mi rey ni otra persona" (p.
1111). In an aside, Marco expresses his admiration for don Juan, who is
like no other *privado*: "este privado / honra de los demás es" (p. 1112).

After much discussion about the love and loyalty of don Juan for his friends, the play comes to an equitable end with the King giving the hand of his sister to his loyal minister, don Juan, thus ensuring his *privanza*. The King also gives the hand of Clavela to don Luis, and promises himself to marry Leonora.

All of the petitions presented by the disguised don Juan can be considered as political commentary on the part of Tirso de Molina. A sovereign should be moderate and prudent by not awarding too many favors, and the royal *privado* should not be given too much power in government matters which are the responsibility of the king. Don Juan is clearly portrayed as the perfect model for all *privado*(s) to follow. He is virtuous, generous, and most important, the King and his nation always come before his personal interests. It is likely that the dramatist aimed to offer Olivares this play as a source of inspiration of ideal behavior on the part of a royal favorite, but, in the words of don Juan, he also warns Philip IV of his responsibilities as king of Castile. Tirso would like to see Philip IV take more personal charge of his government, leaving the royal favorite with less responsibility. This would help to alleviate envy at Court and bring about a healthy body politic.

3. The Theater of Quevedo

Francisco de Quevedo y Villegas (1580–1645) returned from Naples to fix his residence in Spain in 1619.[50] His play *Cómo ha de ser el privado* is an especially good choice for our study not only because, as Melvina Somers states, it is "the only complete extant play by Quevedo,"[51] but also because he was very much a part of seventeenth-century court life.

Miguel Artigas has suggested that this play was written a little before 1628.[52] J.H. Elliott, however, has, with reason, refuted this date because of the reference at the end of the play to Piet Heyn's capture of the Spanish treasure fleet in the fall of 1628, the news of which arrived in Madrid in December of that year. Elliott prefers to accept the date of this play as 1629, since the drama also ends with the celebration of the marriage between the Infanta and the Prince of Transylvania, who is clearly the King of Hungary, to whom the historical Infanta, sister of Philip IV, was in fact married by proxy on April 25, 1629. He believes that Quevedo may have actually written the play expressly for the palace performance in celebration of that marriage.[53]

The play shows the king in a somewhat unfavorable light, as so many of the political plays do, while the *privado* is portrayed as the indispensable center of virtue and efficacy. We are, as in Tirso's *Privar contra su gusto*, introduced to a perfect example of a royal favorite who guides the monarch along the path of uprightness. He illustrates the qualities of total dedication in a *privado* totally lacking in the vice of self-interest. The real figures represented by the characters of the play are very obvious, regardless of the deliberately feeble attempt to conceal their historical identities with the use of anagrams or with fictitious names. The Marquis of *Valisero* is an anagram of the Count-Duke of *Olivares*; the Duke of *Sartabal* is in reality don *Baltasa*r de Zúñiga; the King D. Fernando de Nápoles is Philip IV of Castile; the Infanta Margarita takes the part of the real sister of Philip, the Infanta María; and Carlos, the Prince of Denmark, and the Ambassador of Transylvania are the two suitors who in real life sought her hand in marriage: they were the Prince of Wales and Fernando, the King of Hungary, whom the Infanta married in 1629.[54] The play simply eulogizes the promising administration of Olivares and portrays the ideal *privado* in the person of Valisero.

The play differs from most other dramas of this time since it is almost entirely devoid of conflict in a dramatic sense; its major focus is the portrait of the good *privado*. The king is influenced by the prudent advice of his minister, and the *privado* under no circumstance takes advantage of his position. King Fernando does not fall victim to his passion for the lady Serafina. Adhering to the counsel of his wise favorite, he is able to control his desires, realizing that as a just monarch, he must, for the sake of his country, resist the temptation. The public is left with a total feeling of admiration for the *privado*, whose wise counsel has been the source of royal direction. The plot serves to reenact political occurrences and other incidents of the early years of Philip IV's reign; and the function of these events is to highlight the aspects of a wise and unselfish minister. The main plot, that is, the story of the perfect *privado*, is actually supported by two other intrigues whose function is to emphasize the panegyrical intention of the work. There can be no doubt of this. One of the intrigues used to assist the dramatist in his intention of extolling Olivares as the perfect disinterested minister is the dilemma of the passion that King Fernando feels toward the lady Serafina. The other is the fight for the hand of the Infanta Margarita between the Ambassador of Transylvania and the Prince of Denmark. The main plot therefore is that of the actions of an ideal *privado*, and the other two intrigues are there to exemplify his superior quality as favorite to the King.

The drama begins when the new King requests that three courtiers personally propose a title that would best describe them. One of the responses is that of "fidelity," the next is of "vigilance," and Valisero recommends "disinterest." The King, impressed with the wisdom of the latter, awards the Marquis of Valisero the post as royal *privado*. Valisero illustrates that the only way for a *privado* to fulfill his position completely is through a total disinterest in his own ambitions, giving state matters supreme priority above anything else. This quality of Valisero's is exemplified when he learns of the untimely death of his only son and heir immediately before holding a general audience. Instead of cancelling the audience, Valisero stoically puts this personal tragedy aside, thinking only about the government issues at hand. Quevedo obviously alludes here to the actual death of Olivares's only child, María, in 1626. Although she was his only hope of future family aggrandizement, his continued dedication to a full schedule of activities won him the respect and admiration of many. Personal matters took second place to his responsibility as chief minister of state.[55] Historically his devotion to the public cause was as unrelenting as the one described in the play. In real life, Olivares was described as in "icy self-control" of his emotions and held audiences on the very day of María's death. He acted as a "true neo-Stoic combining classical fortitude with Christian resignation in the tradition of Justus Lipsius."[56] In the play it is not until after the audience that Valisero takes on a more human identity, expressing his sorrow in this way:

> ¿Para qué, Fortuna escasa,
> me diste dichosa suerte,
> si me ha quitado la muerte
> la sucesión de mi casa? [57]

Valisero exemplifies the ideal servant of the state whose disinterest and sense of responsibility are of rare and uncompromising nature. From the beginning of the play, we learn that King Fernando and the lady-in-waiting Serafina are in love. The King must, however, control his desires in order to live according to the standards of his high office. As king he must be a model of uprightness for his subjects to follow. What is most important here is that the King brings his problem directly to his *privado*, who prudently advises him not to run away from it but to face it boldly and to make it plain to Serafina that they can only remain good friends. The King sagaciously heeds the advice of his loyal and wise favorite, and his troubles are over. The monarch therefore does not break the laws of the code of honor, which are deeply rooted in the national consciousness, and the prudent counsel of Valisero is responsible.

It is also through the wise direction and instruction of his *privado* that the play is equitably terminated in yet another respect. Valisero's discretion again comes into play when the King informs his sister Margarita that two suitors wish her hand in marriage. The *privado* bases his counsel on the grounds of religion, and it is his opinion that since the Prince of Denmark is not Catholic and the Ambassador of Transylvania is, she must then marry the latter. As was stated previously, the spread and maintenance of the Catholic faith was one of the major causes of the administration under Olivares. He fought endlessly for Catholic causes in Germany. Elliott also informs us that the Infanta herself had strong negative feelings about marrying a heretic, and that it was Philip himself who ordered Olivares to devise some method to end the marriage plans, since the Prince of Wales refused to be converted to Catholicism. It was this difference in religion which constituted the principal obstacle to their union. Olivares had the difficult task of breaking the engagement tactfully, thus keeping the relations between England and Spain pacific if cool. Spain could in no way afford to enter into war with England at this point.[58] We are led to believe here in this play, through the direction of Quevedo, that it was the wisdom of Olivares which was the decisive factor in the breaking of the marriage plans between the Prince of Denmark and the King's sister Margarita and that an enormous error had consequently been averted.

The philosophy of Bodin states, as we have seen in a previous chapter, that ministers must never overshadow the authority of the monarch. If a king is overridden by passion or forgets the limitations of his office, it is the responsibility of his chief minister, as Bodin explains, to help direct the faltering monarch back on course. Bodin insists, however, as we may recall, that the king's authority is indivisible and absolute and must not be shared with anyone. Quevedo seems to follow this philosophy of Bodin in one of the more poignant scenes of the play. Valisero acts as the spokesman for Quevedo, and sees himself as a tiny atom next to the greatness of his king. His duty is to provide the necessary direction and support to his monarch, but in no way can he actually make royal decisions himself. Quevedo expresses this belief in the words of Valisero:

> Sí, Señor, porque un Privado,
> que es un [átomo pequeño]
> junto al Rey, no ha de ser dueño
> de la luz que el sol le ha dado.
> Es un ministro de ley,
> es un brazo, un instrumento
> por donde pasa el aliento
> a la voluntad del Rey.
> Si dos ángeles ha dado
> Dios al Rey, su parecer
> más acertado ha de ser
> que el parecer del Privado.
> Y así, se debe advertir
> que el Ministro singular
> aunque pueda aconsejar
> no le toca decidir. (pp. 10–11); [emphasis added]

It is more likely that Quevedo intended to illustrate in this play that Olivares had the potential to bring Spain back to her feet again after years of total mismanagement of governmental affairs. The ideal *privado* must, as Quevedo believes of Olivares, possess total dedication to the concerns of the state, leaving his self-interest and ambition behind. He must exhort his monarch to obey the higher laws of nature and of God in which all societies are rooted.

Elliott brings to our attention that Quevedo is able to depict the Count-Duke very accurately. Olivares communicated frequently with other people through letters, and his description of the situation of Spain and of his own personal state bears a close resemblance to the words which Quevedo chooses in the play. For example, Valisero's interpretation of his duties as first minister is a reproduction of Olivares's own ideas of his responsibilities which he expresses in private correspondence. There are many occasions, as Elliott suggests, when reading Quevedo, "one can almost hear Olivares himself speak."[59] What all this means is that Olivares and Quevedo probably shared a close association, or at least a close proximity for an extended period of time. The two men, as Elliott sees it, were both influenced by one another. It seems convincing that Quevedo, with this play, was actually writing a script for Olivares to act out, and which he did very well. Since the attitudes and phraseology of the two are so closely linked, it also suggests that the two men shared a common philosophy, that of Justus Lipsius and neo-stoicism. The influence of Lipsius on the academies and literary circles of early seventeenth-century Seville was great. Olivares enjoyed reading the works of Justus Lipsius as well as Tacitus, all of which indicates that Olivares based the "principles of his life" on Christian stoicism.[60]

It is essential that we keep in mind the events that were taking place around the time of Quevedo's play. At the beginning of the reign of Philip IV and the administration of Olivares, many were eager to believe that this was to be the turning point of the collapsing nation. Quevedo, as well as others, was appalled by the evils of the government established by the authority of self-interested ministers like Lerma and Uceda during the reign of Philip III. Since his youth, Quevedo had always been aware of the problem of the *privado*.[61] Quevedo saw a potential for the reform of Castile in the power of Olivares, whom he believed to be a "good public servant."[62] This play, therefore, which was written in 1629, praises the qualities of leadership in Olivares, since the time of its creation coincides with the first decade of the new administration. Later, however, Quevedo's attitude changed and he began to criticize the Olivares regime.[63]

Melvina Somers sees a close affinity between the play *Cómo ha de ser el privado* and Quevedo's *Política de Dios*.[64] She feels that the real meaning of the play lies in its ideological content, which stems from Quevedo's political philosophy. Christ Himself was the example for monarchs to follow. Both works have, as she states, the didactic purpose of instructing the government and the populace. Interestingly enough, both pieces offer an ideal concept of a ruler and his minister, and both works have Philip IV and Olivares in mind. Somers makes a rather convincing argument that Quevedo utilized dramatic interest in order to advocate a cause in which he believed. A play was certainly a popular form of public entertainment and would reach a much wider audience than a political treatise, which was generally enjoyed only by the intellectually and politically elite. It was his aim, according to Somers, to ennoble the character of the *privado*, who has direct influence on the king. There are also, as she states, parallel passages in the works which urge both Church and State to make a cooperative effort to achieve the ideal Christian government. Quevedo was in strong opposition to the prevalent anti-Christian theories of Machiavelli, against which his *Política de Dios* was a strong "reaction" on behalf of "the Christian ethic."[65]

The importance of the *privado*, as Somers says, is that he must help the king to achieve his true greatness by guiding the king along the path of virtue. Chosen very carefully, he must be a man who is willing to renounce all personal ambition for the sake of his nation. His dedication may at times incur a great deal of suffering, which can only be lightened by the comfort he may find in religion and philosophy. He must never attempt to "override the authority of the king," but also, on the other hand, he must never "indulge the weaknesses" of his sovereign. Always remaining in the background, the *privado* must see to it that the king's will is carried out with the help of his wise counsel. The play actually illustrates how this ideal philosophy can be practiced both by the king and his minister.[66]

To repeat, in the early years of the new government, Quevedo exalted Olivares as the man who would restore Spain to its early greatness. Olivares was a puritanical reformer who refused gifts and favors, whereas in the preceding years Lerma repeatedly accepted them. At the beginning of Philip IV's reign, many men of letters were also quick to make their "obeisance to the men of the new regime," since Olivares not only earned the reputation of being a generous patron to men of learning and letters but also symbolized a change in government and hope for the future. While Olivares ruled the country, he was careful to attract to his company the leading literary, artistic and intellectual figures of the day who were, for personal ambition, eager to depict him as the perfect minister, an image he so badly wanted to convey to the people of Spain. His intention, as the principal minister of the Crown and as a man personally attracted himself to the arts, was to make the Court the focus of literary and artistic patronage in order to show Philip IV as a monarch strong not only in arms but equally as knowlegeable and appreciative of the arts.[67]

Quevedo, like Góngora and many other men of letters in 1621, when young Philip acceded the Crown, was quick to try and please Olivares. On 5 April, for example, only five days after the death of Philip III, Quevedo sent a manuscript of his *Política de Dios* to Olivares and, not wishing to slight Don Baltasar de Zúñiga, he also sent him his "Carta del Rey Don Fernando el Católico," which can be interpreted as either a criticism of the late King Philip III or as an expression of hope that the young monarch would follow the exemplary steps of King Ferdinand.[68] Quevedo was warmly welcomed into the "coterie of court intellectuals" since Olivares, well aware of his reputation for caustic satire, realized that as a man of firm beliefs, Quevedo was not one who was afraid to express his thoughts. Prudently Olivares preferred to have Quevedo on his side rather than on the opposing side of critics. Olivares, with the help of this brillant satirist, was hopeful of creating the perfect image of himself and his King. It is therefore not the least surprising to find Quevedo in the company of the King and his minister on their visits to Andalusia in 1624 and to Aragon in 1626.[69]

The Junta de Reformación, in its attempt to "protect the morals of the young," placed new censorship regulations on the printing of dramas, novels, and other similar works in Castile in the year 1625. Elliott believes that there was an ulterior motive on the part of Olivares behind this ban, which disallowed the printing of almost everything without the prior approval of authorities. He was increasingly more concerned about the growth of literature criticizing the inflation which continued to climb under his government. Even Quevedo was banished in the spring of 1628, but it proved to be a short exile, since he was back again in Madrid in January of 1629. Elliott sees this period after his exile as a time of the "closest association" between Quevedo and Olivares. He believes that the closest advisors of Olivares had probably helped Quevedo back into the circle of those who were committed to the support and defense of Olivares's policies. Hernando de Salazar, the Count-Duke's Jesuit confessor, was probably one of Olivares's emissaries to Quevedo, as was Dr. Alvaro de Villegas, presumed to be a relative of Quevedo's. Another relative of Quevedo's who had strong influence over Olivares was Jerónimo de Villanueva, the Protonotario of the Crown of Aragon, "who by 1629 was already on his way to becoming the right-hand man of Olivares and the second most powerful political figure in Spain." Quevedo's mother died in his earliest years, and as an orphan, he had gone to live with the Villanueva family and therefore came into close contact with Jerónimo de Villanueva, who was fourteen years younger than Quevedo.[70]

In 1629, Olivares also needed the services of Quevedo more than ever before, which may also prove to be a reason for the brevity of Quevedo's banishment from Madrid. Olivares was becoming the target of intense popular hostility, and he needed expert literary help to defend his methods and policies. Inflation continued to soar, Spain's involvement in the War of the Mantuan Succession was turning out to be another disaster, in 1628 the Dutch had seized the Spanish treasure fleet, and in the spring of 1629, he was seen to be in total disagreement as to Spain's foreign policy with both the Council of State and the King himself. Among the chief forces of opposition was Mateo Lisón y Biedma, the representative of Granada in the Cortes of Castile. Three men, however, were most prominent in defense of Olivares and his methods: The Count of La Roca, a friend of Olivares from Seville who had recently finished his manuscript of the *privado*'s biography; Antonio Hurtado de Mendoza, "the house poet of the regime;" and Francisco de Quevedo. Elliott points out the two works written by Quevedo in defense of Olivares which can be dated during this difficult period, the spring or early summer of 1629: the ballad of the "Fiesta de toros literal y alegórica," and the play *Cómo ha de ser el privado*.[71]

To recapitulate, possible motivations behind the writing of this play *Cómo ha de ser el privado* are the following: We can consider it as a piece of propaganda for the regime when Quevedo was still hoping to be accepted into Olivares's close circle of friends. It is a play in which Quevedo, finding Olivares's methods to be a refreshing contrast to those of Lerma, chose to eulogize the new administration. It can also be considered as a piece of laudatory literature paid for by Olivares, who was desperately trying to restore his popularity. We must also consider Somers's theory that the intention of the play was to fulfill the same purpose as that of his political treatise "*Política de Dios,*" which sought to lead the rulers of men to govern by Christian principles. Quevedo believed that the state must have a *privado* whose wise counsel is able to direct the king toward the right path of justice, nobility and wisdom. In effect, Quevedo wished to urge his government to model its actions on the conduct of Christ. And lastly, as Elliott suggests, the play was perhaps created by Quevedo in order to curtail the exile to which he was sentenced in 1628.

We have now looked at several dramas of marked political content, though diverse in orientation, in the theater of Lope, Tirso, and Quevedo. Politics and government are not major themes in the repertoire of either Lope or Tirso, but when they appear, Lope generally focuses on the glory and wisdom of monarchs, whereas Tirso views the king and his ministers with considerable suspicion and finds hope only in discovering the rare disinterested *privado* who shuns self-glorification. Quevedo's one essay into political theater likewise focuses on the absolute necessity of a disciplined and self-sacrificial first minister. None of these playwrights gives us dramas which examine persistently how an absolutist system works and what steps must and can be taken against a tyrannical monarch—i.e., available *political* measures, beyond simple reliance on the moral goodness of the *privado*, which the state has within its arsenal. We now turn to the political drama of Juan Ruiz de Alarcón, who is as insistent on virtue and morality as any of his contemporaries but also attentive, as they are not, to brakes on human passion and corruption built into the system of government. Steadier and more constant in his plays also is the consideration of economic and social malfunctions in the Spanish society of his day.

NOTES

[1] José Antonio Maravall, *Teatro y literatura en la sociedad barroca* (Madrid: Seminarios y Ediciones, S.A., 1972), pp. 21–22.

[2] Díez Borque, *Sociología de la comedia española del siglo XVII* (Madrid: Ediciones Cátedra, S.A., 1976), p. 131; see also Maravall, p. 21.

[3] Díez Borque, p. 174.

[4] Maravall, p. 22.

[5] Maravall, p. 25.

[6] Maravall, p. 29.

[7] Maravall, p. 31.

[8] Díez Borque, p. 310.

[9] Maravall, p. 65.

[10] Maravall, pp. 70–71.

[11] Maravall, pp. 65–77.

[12] Ruth Lee Kennedy, *Studies in Tirso,* vol. 1 (Chapel Hill, N.C.: U of North Carolina P, 1974), p. 37.

[13] Leicester Bradner, "The Theme of Privanza in Spanish and English Drama," in *Homenaje a William L. Fichter*, (Madrid: Editorial Castalia, 1971), p. 106.

[14] Bradner, p. 100.

[15] Bradner, p. 103.

[16] Kennedy, pp. 36–37.

17 Díez Borque, pp. 141–143.

18 Maravall, p. 78.

19 Kennedy, p. 37.

20 Díez Borque, p. 130.

21 Maravall, p. 54.

22 Díez Borque, pp. 130–152.

23 Díez Borque, p. 141, quoted from G. González de Amezúa, *Epistolario*, IV, p. 104.

24 S. Griswold Morley and Courtney Bruerton, *Cronología de las comedias de Lope de Vega* (Madrid: Editorial Gredos, S.A., 1968), p. 68.

25 Díez Borque, p. 147.

26 Díez Borque, p. 147.

27 Morley and Bruerton, p. 70.

28 Morley and Bruerton, p. 70.

29 Díez Borque, p. 149–150.

30 Díez Borque, pp. 152–160.

31 Kennedy, p. 61.

32 Kennedy, pp. 61–62.

33 Kennedy, p. 13.

34 Kennedy, p. 190.

35 Kennedy, p. 355.

36 Kennedy, p. 148.

37 Kennedy, p. 99.

38 Blanca de los Ríos, "Preámbulo" to *La prudencia en la mujer* in *Obras dramáticas completas*, vol. 3, ed. Blanca de los Ríos (Madrid: Aguilar, 1958), p. 895.

39 Blanca de los Ríos, "Preámbulo," pp. 895–896.

40 Blanca de los Ríos, "Preámbulo," pp. 896–897.

41 Tirso de Molina, *La prudencia en la mujer* in *Obras dramáticas completas*, vol. 3, ed. Blanca de los Ríos (Madrid: Aguilar, 1958), p. 909. (All further citations of this play refer to this edition.)

42 Kennedy, pp. 11–13.

43 Kennedy, pp. 248–249 n.5.

44 Blanca de los Ríos, "Preámbulo" to *Privar contra su gusto* in *Obras dramáticas completas*, vol. 3, ed. Blanca de los Ríos (Madrid:Aguilar, 1958), p. 1070.

45 Blanca de los Ríos, "Preámbulo," pp. 1069–1070.

46 Blanca de los Ríos, "Preámbulo," p. 1072.

[47] Blanca de los Ríos, "Preámbulo," pp. 1069–1075.

[48] Kennedy, pp. 354–356.

[49] Tirso de Molina, *Privar contra su gusto* in *Obras dramáticas completas*, vol. 3, ed. Blanca de los Ríos (Madrid: Aguilar, 1958), pp. 1075–1076. (All further citations of this play refer to this edition.)

[50] José Manuel Blecua, "Introducción" to *Obras Completas.* vol. 1: *Poesía original*, by Francisco de Quevedo (Barcelona: Planeta, 1963), pp. xxxi–xxxvi.

[51] Melvina Somers, "Quevedo's Ideology in *Cómo ha de ser el Privado*," *Hispania*, 39 (1956), p. 261.

[52] Miguel Artigas, "Introducción" to *Teatro Inédito de Don Francisco de Quevedo y Villegas* (Madrid: Real Academia Española, 1927) , p. xvii.

[53] J.H. Elliott, "Quevedo and the Count-Duke of Olivares," in *Quevedo in Perspective*, ed. James Iffland (Delaware: Juan de la Cuesta, 1982), p. 235.

[54] Artigas, "Introducción," pp. xvii–xviii.

[55] Elliott, *The Count-Duke*, pp. 280–281.

[56] Elliott, *The Count-Duke*, p. 280.

[57] Francisco de Quevedo y Villegas, *Cómo ha de ser el privado* in *Teatro inédito de Don Francisco de Quevedo y Villegas* (Madrid: Tipografía de la "Revista de Archivos," 1927), p. 49. (All further citations of this play refer to this edition.)

[58] Elliott, *The Count-Duke*, pp. 204–214.

[59] Elliott, "Quevedo and the Count-Duke of Olivares," p. 237.

[60] Elliott, "Quevedo and the Count-Duke of Olivares," pp. 237–239.

[61] Somers, p. 261.

[62] Somers, p. 261.

[63] Elliott suggests that the relationship between Quevedo and Olivares remained excellent until at least the end of 1634. He detects the first signs of Quevedo's general alienation from the Olivares regime between the years 1634–1635, when he turned into a strong opponent of Olivares and his policies. "Quevedo and the Count-Duke of Olivares," pp. 241–42.

[64] Somers, p. 261.

[65] Somers, pp. 261–262.

[66] Somers, pp. 261–268.

[67] Elliott, "Quevedo and the Count-Duke of Olivares," pp. 228–230.

[68] Elliott, "Quevedo and the Count-Duke of Olivares," pp. 228–229.

[69] Elliott, "Quevedo and the Count-Duke of Olivares," p. 231.

[70] Elliott, "Quevedo and the Count-Duke of Olivares," pp. 231–233.

[71] Elliott, "Quevedo and the Count-Duke of Olivares," pp. 231–234.

CHAPTER V
THE POLITICAL PLAYS OF JUAN RUIZ DE ALARCÓN

Born in 1580 or 1581 in the City of Mexico, Ruiz de Alarcón studied law at the University of Mexico and went to Spain in 1600 to continue his legal studies at the University of Salamanca, from which he received the degree of Bachelor of Canon Law in 1600 and that of Bachelor of Civil Law in 1602. He continued studies at Salamanca probably until 1606, when he moved to Seville and practiced law. In 1608 he returned to Mexico, where after receiving the degree of Licentiate in Civil and Canon Law in 1609, he practiced law until his return to Spain in 1613. Living in Madrid, he soon became a well-known figure in literary circles and academies. His plays were being performed in public theaters and at Court with frequency between the years of 1618 and 1627; but it is clear that his major goal was an appointment to a position in the government for which his extensive legal training qualified him.

In 1626 he was finally appointed as a supernumerary *relator* (court reporter) on the Council of the Indies and in 1633 was designated as one of the three official *relatores* on the Council. The *relator* was perhaps the Council member who worked the hardest and most constantly, summarizing all the letters and documents that flowed in from the Indies. They were sworn to absolute secrecy about the documents in their hands and could not delegate any of the mass of work before them to secretaries or scribes. In these circumstances it was impossible for Alarcón to continue to write much, if at all, for the theaters. He largely exchanged the company of poets and playwrights for that of lawyers and bureaucrats, perhaps with a feeling of relief, since his Mexican origin and the highly visible hump on his back had all too often moved the writers' sharp tongues to cruel jokes and satire.[1]

Alarcón is known to literary history primarily for his comedias of customs and manners, such as *La verdad sospechosa* and *Las paredes oyen*. Relatively little attention has been given to another group of plays (six of the twenty published by him during his lifetime, and one of the three others commonly attributed to him) which treat the nature of kingship, the function and character of the *privado*, the vital importance of respect for, and adherence to the nation's laws, and the suggestion of new policies and laws to promote public welfare.

These are the plays I propose to study here: *Los favores del mundo, Los pechos privilegiados, El dueño de las estrellas, La amistad castigada, Ganar amigos, La crueldad por el honor,* and *No hay mal que por bien no venga.* In the first five the central plot treats the relationships between the king and his *privado*; in the last two the citizen's duty to a sovereign threatened with revolt provides the major thematic interest.

For obvious reasons (see above, Ch.II) the *privado* became an interesting figure to seventeenth-century dramatists. Almost all of them wrote one or several dramas in which he plays a prominent role. Lope wrote ten such plays, Montalbán composed seven,[2] and we have already studied two such plays by Tirso and one by Quevedo. Still, it is Alarcón who was visibly most interested in this new political phenomenon, for five (or a quarter) of the 20 plays surely by him deal with *privado*(s), good, bad, failed or successful.[3]

Alarcón, like Tirso and others, dared to present evil *privado*(s) on the stage, as well as evil kings who abused the law by attacking women's honor. Royal or *privado* abuses are transformed in his plays primarily into attacks on women. It seems incredible that Alarcón, who had been seeking a government post since his second arrival in Spain in 1613, would dare to antagonize the administration with political plays of this nature, performed between ca. 1616 and 1625, the time span covering the end of Philip III's reign and the beginning years of the new regime under Olivares.

In some measure the dramatist protected himself by setting all these plays in remote times and/or remote countries, making it possible to claim no critical intention about the contemporary Spanish monarch or *privado.* Yet the historical disguise is usually very thin and ripped apart at times by violent anachronisms. His intention was to educate his audience in the importance of some moral truth or political or economic conviction, and perhaps he felt he could better control this educational environment if he could use history to suit his purpose rather than attempting to recreate faithfully a past time and another country. Indeed, the term "historical play" in this epoch may be a "misnomer": A. Robert Lauer suggests that it is a work which "uses historical personages (or names) for the poet's aesthetic, moral, or political intentions."[4]

Alarcón has done precisely this. He chose to manipulate history to the needs and design of the play and to accomplish what Lindenberger calls "the translation of a historical source into a contemporary dramatic convention."[5] Lauer states that a poet may choose to recast history for his own purposes but adds that when a poet reaches this level of "flux and sublimation, one can say that the poet not merely uses but abuses history."[6] The real value of a historical play, in Lauer's opinion, lies in the variations introduced into a well-known historical account. An artist infuses greater meaning into his work when he puts aside the concern for historical accuracy, and emphasizes something of greater importance instead.[7]

National history, as Alarcón knew well, enjoys a special dignity in the theater in general, and so does ancient Roman and Greek history. Lindenberger suggests that ancient history is a part of the "national consciousness of all modern Europe."[8] It was, however, especially important to Alarcón, whose concern to educate his audience far surpassed any inclination toward historical accuracy; the significant dramatic effect desired is to have the audience feel a continuity between the present and the past. This "historical continuity,"[9] as Lindenberger calls it, has a real value. The employment of the history of the ancient Roman Empire, for example, endows the history of Spain, considered to be the inheritor of Roman imperial tradition, with a special degree of dignity.[10] Therefore, by employing ancient history or personages in his plays, Alarcón was able to ennoble his dramas in order to present his message with maximum force.

It is also interesting to note that Alarcón's works are filled with characteristics typical of his professions as lawyer, jurist and *relator*,[11] the position which he assumed on the Council of the Indies in June of 1626. His plays are obsessed with the importance of truth and the observance of secrecy,[12] and "todo lo característico en el teatro de Alarcón es, evidentemente, la moral de un relator."[13] Alcalá-Zamora says that the spirit of Alarcón "afirma la primacía del derecho."[14] Even though most, if not all of his plays, were written before 1626 and his assumption of the duties of a *relator*, his extensive legal training and the desire to impress the administration with his professionalism undoubtedly explains in part the emphasis on law in his plays.

A. *Privado*-King plays

1. Los favores del mundo

Los favores del mundo, composed as early as 1616,[15] was played in Madrid on 3 February, 1618.[16] It can be conjectured that Alarcón wrote the play during the final years of the reign of the frail monarch Philip III, who relied completely upon his *privado* Lerma to run the government of the nation, partially in order to illustrate to the young Prince Philip that all *privado*(s) need not conform to Lerma's pattern.

The drama takes place in medieval Madrid in the year 1448 during the reign of John II, but it deals primarily with his son, the future Henry IV, who "había comenzado ya a prodigar tierras y favores a vasallos afortunados..."[17] The ambiance of the action is, however, really Philip III's Madrid, which is described by Garci-Ruiz in the opening lines of the play as the "corte del Rey de España," which it was not in 1448 and did not become until the mid-sixteenth century.

The first act is devoted to the development of Garci-Ruiz's character and to highlighting his uniqueness as a Spanish courtier. He comes to Madrid in order to avenge an affront committed by a certain don Juan some time before. Don Juan apparently dishonored Garci-Ruiz by calling him a coward in battle (vss. 541–544). [18]

Alarcón is original in his divergence from the necessity of revenge evident in many seventeenth-century dramas. In general, in order to restore honor and order in society, one must avenge an offense. Alarcón, however, softens the severity of this social code perhaps in order to criticize the harshness of revenge so prevalent in contemporary Spanish theater. "El honor fue la piedra angular en la vida del XVII, que afectó a la vida religiosa, económica, cultural, familiar...hasta convertirse en la razón activa del existir de los personajes."[19] When Garci-Ruiz finally meets up with his offender, don Juan de Luna, for whom he has searched a long while, he finds he has conquered the desire to avenge himself and cannot kill his antagonist when the latter invokes the aid of the Virgin. Garci-Ruiz has achieved an important victory over himself and the traditional precepts of society rather than over his enemy. He is, as Alarcón intended, a unique seventeenth-century Spanish courtier whose sense of justice does not allow him to avenge the affront with the death of the offender, and here is precisely where Alarcón's originality lies. The rigidity of the honor code is softened by the portrayal of a heroic character who is capable of forgiveness. His honor is satisfied more in the act of pardoning than in the act of cold-blooded murder, and he is content being true to himself by ignoring the generally accepted ways of society (vss. 192–204). Alcalá-Zamora suggests that Alarcón, because of his preoccupation with morality, has frequently included the act of pardon in order to resolve penal problems.[20] Considering the numerous occasions on which Alarcón's characters exercise this new tempered justice, it is probable that the intention of the dramatist was to convince his audience that it is not always wise to endorse the austere, although customary, practices of the contemporary society .

Garci-Ruiz is the key element in the education of Prince Henry. The Prince is impressed by his clemency and praises Garci-Ruiz by saying that his valor lies in the fact that he did not kill don Juan (who is, coincidentally, the Prince's *privado*). Such a murder, the Prince also now sees, through the example of Garci-Ruiz, would be rash and violent. True and lasting victory, he says, lies in forgiveness (vss. 602–660). The Prince requests that Garci-Ruiz remain with him as a *privado*, since he is eager to learn from him the true meaning of piety and valor (vss. 686–690). His speech is a clearly presented lawyer's statement of the advantages of pardon over reparation of honor by the death of the offender.

Garci-Ruiz again proves his singularity by the fact that he really does not desire the newly awarded post as *privado*. Unlike other courtiers who would do anything for the opportunity, he sees more reward in acts of mercy than in the glorified position of *privado* (vss. 789–794). Garci-Ruiz is, however, a loyal subject and does agree to remain at Court. Don Juan in Tirso's drama *Privar contra su gusto* similarly assumes the position of *privado* with reluctance.

Prince Henry now has two *privado*(s), Juan de Luna and Garci-Ruiz, and both are admirable men. Such a position would perhaps be better filled by two men rather than just one. This seems to be the dramatist's belief since the Prince tells don Juan that as God had many favorites, the king will also have more than one (vss. 1101–1104). Juan is unmoved by greed and ambition when the Prince asks Garci-Ruiz to aid him in government affairs as his other *privado*. He acknowledges the wisdom of Garci-Ruiz and realizes that the administration of a nation is no simple matter, and to obey the wishes of the Prince is the highest priority in his hierarchy of values. In the final act of the play, as we will see, he is faced with another dilemma when forced to choose between his friendship with Garci-Ruiz and loyalty to the Prince. In the end he decides that loyalty to the king must always take precedence over friendship, and friendship must always come before love.

Alarcón has deliberately presented Garci-Ruiz and don Juan as prototypes of a new wave of *privado*(s). The administration of Lerma (see Ch.II above) was corrupt. Lerma and his underlings utilized the treasury of the monarchy for their own personal advantage with no regard for their country as a whole or for morality. Garci-Ruiz and don Juan, on the other hand, are portrayed as different from the rest; they are men who can recognize right from wrong and choose morality over all.

The first act establishes a love intrigue based on the Prince's attraction to Anarda, Count Mauricio's lust for her, and Anarda and Garci-Ruiz's deep love for each other, all of which adds to Garci-Ruiz's conflicts throughout the play. As an added complication, don Juan also reveals his love for Anarda's cousin Julia.

In the second act, the Prince and his *privado*, don Juan, greet Garci-Ruiz warmly, since they are delighted to have such a virtuous man in their midst. He has, during his short stay, already been a source of inspiration to the Court as a model of forgiveness. He has introduced a new wave of justice which is tempered with clemency, the kind of justice which Alarcón no doubt admired.

In this same act, Garci-Ruiz learns that both he and the Prince are in love with the same woman, Anarda. He feels trapped, since the love he has for her is fruitless. He curses his appointment as *privado* to the Prince, seeing all the royal favors and honor as nothing when compared to love (vss. 1195–1200). Like Don Juan, however, he feels bound by loyalty to his Prince to give up his love; the Prince is his sovereign, to whom he owes loyalty, so that "venza al amor la lealtad" (vs.1239). Here again we are reminded of the anguish experienced by don Juan in Tirso's *Privar contra su gusto*, who sacrifices his love for the king's sister, since his concern for state matters far exceeds his personal desires for the love of a woman.

Feeling a strain upon the friendship which he and the Prince share, Garci-Ruiz decides to leave Court in order not to hinder the possible relationship between Prince Henry and Anarda. Anarda, however, has fallen passionately in love with Garci-Ruiz and remains so throughout the remainder of the play.

Garci-Ruiz is again placed into a precarious situation with the Prince in this act. As requested by Henry, Garci-Ruiz keeps watch over Anarda's street in order to protect her honor and the interests of the Prince. In order to obey Henry's wishes, Garci-Ruiz is forced to risk his own life in a sword fight which ends with Garci-Ruiz wounding Count Mauricio, who, moved by lustful desires for Anarda, has attempted to enter her house. The Prince, however, is angered by his *privado*'s action against Mauricio, who is one of his ministers, and Garci-Ruiz is released from his post. Garci-Ruiz, presented as a man faithful to the teachings of Bodin, according to which a subject must always be obedient to his king, accepts dismissal without protest.

Prince Henry, who is at the axis of the plot, is not a king. Perhaps Alarcón was offering young Prince Philip, the future Philip IV, an example of perfect *privado*(s) whose loyalty to the Crown is unswerving, or perhaps the dramatist was protecting himself from royal censure by avoiding the placement of a king on the stage who does not appreciate the loyalty of his subjects. In general, Spanish theater has advocated loyalty to one's sovereign in Bodinian fashion, but in this drama, Alarcón suggests that Garci-Ruiz's sure sense of right and wrong is not appreciated by the Prince. Lope de Vega's plays, for example, have been seen as the epitome of such loyalty to absolutism,[21] the mentality of "la religión de la obediencia" seen in dramatists especially during the reign of Philip IV. [22] It seems unjust here, however, that Garci-Ruiz is left with the shame of having lost his court position when he was only obeying the Prince's own orders. In trying to please the Prince, he instead offends him. Alarcón leads the spectator and the reader to question the justice of a system in which a loyal *privado* is dismissed for his act of obedience. Garci-Ruiz himself remarks that his error was to have obeyed (vs. 1593). The fallen *privado* then agonizes over his disgrace and wonders whether being a *privado* is worth the trouble and heartbreaks he must now bear (vss. 1597–1600). We admire him precisely because he has obeyed, and we are led to question the behavior of a sovereign who gives an order (in other words, issues a decree or law) and then does not sustain it. The word of a king is law, and it is suggested even the king must respect it. Both Bodin and Mariana roughly coincide in this opinion.

Garci-Ruiz also is troubled by the instability of life and love. He finds that the personality of the Prince wavers from kindness to meanness from one day to the next, he falls in love with Anarda one day and loses all hope of having her the next, and finally he gains and loses the favor of the Prince in an equally abrupt changing of the tides (vss. 1600–1628). He begs for the necessary patience to survive this hell of fear and anxiety which are "los favores del mundo" (vss. 1629–1632).

Don Juan is a noble character who intercedes on behalf of Garci-Ruiz. The bond of friendship formed between the two men after their duel is lasting, unlike everything else in the *privado*'s life. Don Juan prudently advises the Prince not to ill-treat the fallen *privado* since he remembers only too well that it was Garci-Ruiz who forgave and spared him his life. The uprightness of Garci-Ruiz has been a good influence upon the entire Court, and this act of intercession is proof of the lasting virtue which don Juan has acquired from Garci-Ruiz. It is precisely the lasting virtue that Garci-Ruiz exemplifies and inspires in others, together with the bond of friendship which has been cemented between the two courtiers, which Alarcón intends to underscore and to contrast with the inconstancy of earthly pleasures and favors. The presentation of ideal *privado*(s) who counsel the king wisely and become a source of inspiration to the ministers at Court anticipates the situation in the play *Ganar amigos*, which will be examined later.

The Prince, having learned clemency from his fallen *privado*, and counseled by don Juan, finally consents to the marriage of Anarda and Garci-Ruiz after Garci-Ruiz, like a clever lawyer, uses the Prince's own words to trap him into marrying Anarda to him and not to Count Mauricio, as the Prince had planned. Since Henry has referred to Garci-Ruiz as his best friend and his *privado mayor* (vss. 3216–3219), the latter subsequently confronts the Prince with these very words:

> pero si habéis dicho vos
> que vuestro mayor amigo
> y mayor privado soy,
> lo que dábades al Conde,
> ¿cómo puedo pensar yo
> que me lo neguéis a mí? (vss. 3227–3232)

Though Henry protests against the "sofísticos argumentos" of Garci-Ruiz (vs. 3234), he accepts the legal defeat and Garci-Ruiz is once again established as his *privado*.

Alarcón was well read in all the reform literature as well as the poltical treatises of his day. He was, therefore, very aware of the conditions surrounding him and did not hesitate to criticize what he believed to be some of the causes of the social and economic decline. The *gracioso*, Hernando, is the spokesman for a good part of this criticism. He is amazed that Anarda addresses him as a *caballero* but understands her error since "...no soy el primero / que en la corte se trasforma" (vss. 327–328).

Hernando's satire lengthens as he cautions Anarda about the lack of genuineness at Court. There is, he says, always an evil motive behind every kiss (vss. 368–372). He also pokes fun at the Spanish courtier whose sole motivation is money (vss. 395–396). The satire on the drive for money continues in the words of Anarda's uncle, who encourages her to marry Count Mauricio, a well-to-do gentleman who can offer her a prosperous future (vs. 1665). What are the priorities of court life? The play chides Spanish society for having placed too much emphasis on the importance of having money and on the over-ambitious and immoral tactics that are used in order to get it. This play, anticipating the Junta de Reformación of the Olivares administration and composed a little before—and performed around the time of—the appearance of Pérez de Herrera's *Proverbios morales y consejos cristianos*, is averse to ostentatious spending. Pérez de Herrera was opposed to the superflous amount of money spent on clothing, servants and food (see Ch.III, p. 28). Later the Junta (see Ch.III, p. 33), influenced by proposals of Pérez de Herrera, requested that the nobility return to their country estates, and thus cut down on the excessive spending of the nobility on items such as clothing, furnishings and jewelry.

In the final act, Hernando gives a lengthy exposition of the shocking morality of court life. Because Spanish courtiers are monetarily motivated, people's values have become twisted. In order to be accepted, one must possess money; the outcasts are the have-nots. The poor man is unable to accomplish his ambitions, and the rich have no ambition which will benefit the nation. He warns that one would have to be crazy to want to come to Madrid to live with this kind of mentality (vss. 2586–2599). Garci-Ruiz considers leaving the Court to return to his country estate. Hernando continues his bitter criticism of life at Court, saying that everything here is either a form of fraud, deception or trickery (vss. 2630–2631).

Anarda's uncle is angered by her refusal to wed the Count and threatens to put her in a convent if she does not obey his wishes. She, however, a typical Alarconian heroine, is a liberated woman, unique in her independence, and refuses to listen to him, retorting that marriage and religion have to be of her own choice (vss. 1718–1722). She even decides to run away from Court before she is pressed into marriage with a man she does not love or forced into a convent when she lacks a true vocation (vss. 3024–3047). She does not sit back and allow her male family members to decide her future for her. She is intelligent and decisive.[23] Her words illustrate Alarcón's disdain of forced marriages. Marriages, if they are to be happy, cannot be forced. A harmonious union is one of choice by both partners. This strong-minded woman also directs criticism at the false flattery prevalent at Court. Unsure of Garci-Ruiz's true feelings for her, she tells him that she prefers to hear the cold, hard truth rather than hear the customary court flattery. (vss. 1987–1990).

It is logical that with this play, though ostensibly set in 1448, the playwright's intention was to offer to the young Prince Philip in 1616–1618 examples of ideal *privado*(s), especially during the time when the image of the royal *privado* had become so twisted by the abusive control of the Lerma regime. Another intention perhaps was to instruct the young Prince in the importance of a clement sense of justice. When Garci-Ruiz conquers his anger towards don Juan, he achieves an even greater victory over himself and over the commonly accepted precepts of the contemporary society. Because of the compassion displayed by the protagonist, *Los favores del mundo* is a unique play which tempers the old precepts with a more lenient sense of justice. Don Juan, the other *privado*, must also be regarded with respect. His wise counsel and support of the Prince largely contribute to the ordered justice at the end of the play.

2. El dueño de las estrellas

El dueño de las estrellas was composed, according to Bruerton, between the years 1620?–1623?, which embrace the time of Philip III's death and the accession to the throne of the young Philip IV on 31 March, 1621.

The play takes place in ancient Crete, but, as in all of his works, Alarcón uses this setting as a figleaf hiding a seventeenth-century Spanish world. He chooses to deform historical accuracy in this play in order to utilize the character of Lycurgus, the famous Spartan lawgiver, about whom very little is known. Our few notions of Lycurgus have mainly come from Plutarch, who explains that "we have nothing to relate that is certain and uncontroverted. For there are different accounts of his birth, his travels, his death, and especially of the laws and form of government, which he established."[24] Plutarch places his birth at 926 B.C. and adds that his code of laws was established at Lacedaemon in 884 B.C.[25] Plutarch further explains how Lycurgus acquired the throne. The lenient King Eurytion had relaxed the strictness of kingly government, and, as a result, Sparta was in a state of anarchy and confusion. A later king, Lycurgus's father, was killed and left the throne to his eldest son. Soon after, this young king also died, and the general voice elected Lycurgus to the throne. He accepted the position but his rule was short-lived (a span of only eight months), since he discovered that his brother's widow was pregnant and insisted that the rightful king was his brother's child, so long as it was a male offspring. Lycurgus wished to remain only as his guardian and to help direct the administration. The citizens of Sparta, however, had come to admire Lycurgus for his virtue, and were always ready to execute his commands. It was the will of Lycurgus, however, that the young king Charilaus, "chara" meaning "joy," be left in command. Lycurgus, as a result of some contention which arose out of jealousy toward him, decided to leave Sparta and travel to other countries to gain political knowledge and experience. [26]

Alarcón undoubtedly used Plutarch's *Lives* as a source of information, since in the play the Alarconian Lycurgus gives an almost identical account to the king of Crete of his accession to the throne with some slight variation for the purpose of simplicity (vss. 990–1139).[27]

There are other aspects of Plutarch's account of Lycurgus which are perhaps pertinent to this study. Plutarch explains that he went to the island of Crete, where he came to admire some of the Cretans' laws and resolved to bring their ideas back to Sparta. In Crete, Lycurgus also met one of the seven wise men of Greece, Thales, who was a poet and a musician and famed as an excellent lawgiver. It was Thales who prepared the way for Lycurgus toward the instruction of the Spartans. Traveling onward, Lycurgus saw the contrast between the luxury and expense which the Ionians were known for and the frugality and spare diets of the Cretans. After comparing the two distinct forms of life, he was able to ascertain the effect each produced on the manners and government of the people and decided that a simple and disciplined way of life was beneficial. In Asia Minor Lycurgus also learned of Homer's poems, which were intermixed with moral statements and political knowledge. In Egypt, Lycurgus was most pleased with the strength of the military. The

Lacedaemonians then begged Lycurgus to return to Sparta, realizing that no one else had the ability to rule as he did.[28] Plutarch explains that "Lycurgus had a natural ability to guide the measures of government, and powers of persuasion which won the human heart."[29] Lycurgus, who resolved to alter the whole framework of the constitution of Sparta, preferred that his laws never be written down. Instead, he wanted the "principles of his policy" to be a part of the education of the youth.[30] "For what he thought most conducive to the virtue and happiness of a city, was principle interwoven with the manners and breeding of the people."[31] Even matters of lesser importance were never written down in an unalterable form, since he felt that time must allow for certain changes.[32] Plutarch describes Lycurgus as the author of a wholly new set of laws and institutions. It is pertinent to examine some of these laws and institutions of Lycurgus in this study to see what effect they may have had on Alarcón's thought.

The first and most important institution which Lycurgus established was the senate. This twenty-eight man senate was given the authority to share in the power of the king in order to keep the sometimes imperious king within the bounds of moderation and to preserve the state. The senate's job was to maintain a just equilibrium between the king and the people, making certain to adhere to the king "whenever they saw the people too encroaching, and on the other hand supporting the people, when the kings attempted to make themselves absolute."[33]

He also attempted to equalize the wealth of the citizens of Sparta in a number of ways. He cancelled all former divisions of land and made new ones, he rid the city of its gold and silver and made use of an iron currency instead, and he banned all unprofitable and superfluous arts, in the attempt to exterminate the love of riches and to equalize the people. His purpose was to unite them, thus creating a stronger city whose citizens' main concern would not be for themselves as individuals but for their country as a whole. Another institution which Lycurgus established in order to unite the people of Sparta was public dining halls where rich and poor, adults and children, dined together. Lycurgus also attempted to banish unnecessary splendor and luxury in the home, in the hope that Spartan life would be roughly equal for all. Excellent workmanship in useful and necessary items was emphasized instead.

Other ordinances which Lycurgus deemed necessary were the following: that the Spartans should not make war on the same enemy twice since repeated engagements only improve the fighting ability of their opponents. He looked upon the education of the youth of Sparta as his main concern and encouraged exercise and discipline for both male and female adolescents. He believed that their education was an exercise in obedience and enrolled all seven-year-old males in special companies where they received a lean diet and learned to be subject to command, to fight, endure and to conquer. He considered children more the property of the state than of the parents, and young women were encouraged to unite with men of breeding in order to give offspring who would benefit the state.[34] No man was "at liberty to live as he pleased, the city being like one great camp, where all had their stated allowance and knew their public charge; each man concluding that he was born not for himself but for his country."[35] Lycurgus encouraged the enjoyment of leisure, thus leaving any mechanical trade to the Helot slaves. He was, however, averse to loitering and wasting valuable time. He promoted constructive use of free time in schools and in places of conversation.[36] He wanted the Spartans to behave in the manner of bees that "acted with one impulse for the public good, and always assembled about their prince."[37] Lycurgus also ordered that all dead be buried in the city in order to acquaint the young with death at an early age. He also prohibited his countrymen from going abroad to visit other countries, "lest they should contract foreign manners, a proneness to imitate the undisciplined, and a variety of opinions upon government."[38] With the same concern, he excluded strangers from entering Sparta who had not come for a particularly beneficial reason.

After proving himself to be, as Plutarch describes, a leader of "mildness and justice,"[39] Lycurgus decided to visit Delphi in order to consult the oracle and to ask Apollo if his laws were sufficient to promote virtue and secure a happy and healthy body politic. He told his countrymen to observe his laws, without modification, until his return and they so swore. According to Plutarch, the answer which Apollo gave to Lycurgus, who wrote it down and sent it to Sparta, was as follows: "The laws were excellent, and that the city which adhered to the constitution he had established, would be the most glorious in the world."[40] It has been said that Lycurgus then killed himself in order to prevent his return to Sparta, realizing that if he never returned, his countrymen would continue to abide by his laws, as they had promised they would do in his absence. Sparta, as Lycurgus had hoped, continued to be superior to the rest of Greece, "both in its government at home and its reputation abroad, so long as it retained the institutions of Lycurgus; and this it did during the space of five hundred years, and the reign of fourteen successive kings down to Agis the son of Archidamus."[41] Throughout history, the Sparta of Lycurgus was famed as a "school of discipline, where the beauty of life and political order were taught in the utmost perfection."[42]

El dueño de las estrellas was probably written during the very first years of the reign of Philip IV and at the time when the Count of Olivares was cementing his position as *privado* and laying plans for reform of the economy and the bolstering of national morals. It was a good time to dramatize the life of a renowned reforming lawgiver who, according to legend, had established Sparta as a great state. In the opening lines of the play, the young and inexperienced King of Crete, "yo en la edad de joven floreciente" (vs. 10) comes to ask the Delphic oracle what he must do to "reinar en paz" (so much the need of the Spanish state). He is told that he should seek Lycurgus the olive tree (interpreted as Lycurgus's laws), for "no hay árbol para un reino más dichoso / que el de la oliva, porque paz publica" (vss. 51–52). This *árbol venturoso* (vs. 17), *la oliva*, is the symbol of peace and law, and is also an obvious allusion to the name *Olivares*. In other words the young Cretan king should reign with the help of Lycurgus the lawgiver, whose counsel will assure peace. For any moderately alert spectator, this scene implies that young Philip IV should seek the counsel of the Count of Olivares in order to achieve a reign of peace. There is also another hint which invites the reader to believe that Alarcón's Lycurgus is in actuality Olivares. Later in Act I, Severo describes Lycurgus as a man who "con pasión / natural inclinación / a letras y armas mostráis" (vss. 430–432). Elliott also informs us that Olivares had a natural passion for books and was a collector of rare and distinguished writings. It was probably during the Seville years that Don Gaspar began to build up what came to be known as one of the most impressive libraries in seventeenth-century Europe.[43] At the same time Olivares took great pride in the military strength of his nation, so important for the defense of the country. In the end, ironically, Olivares, the man bearing the olive branch of peace, would advocate war "to renew and regenerate the Spanish monarchy."[44]

Lycurgus has come to Crete, where he lives in hiding, disguised as the peasant Lacón, until he is discovered by the King's wise old counselor Severo. However, before he is found, Lycurgus becomes involved in a quarrel between the *gracioso*, Coridón, and a courtier, Teón, who attempts to take advantage of Coridón's wife. Lycurgus comes to the aid of Coridón and is insulted by Teón. Lycurgus, very much a seventeenth-century courtier, is attentive to his honor and vows to take revenge on Teón for the insult.

When Lycurgus comes to the Court, he is greeted with more honor and dignity than he deems necessary, since he comes as a vassal to serve the king with no reward in mind (vss. 940–943). The intention was to portray a favorable image of Olivares as a dedicated man whose one goal in life was to serve his king and his nation without self-interest. It was his desire to be regarded simply as "the king's faithful servant."[45] The King of Crete recognizes that although he wears the crown, he needs the assistance of the Spartan lawgiver Lycurgus and begs him to be his *privado*, a position which Lycurgus warns the King he should not accept, since it has been forcasted that he will either kill or be killed by a king (vss. 1114–1115). The King, however, is not a superstitious man and, driven by desperation to cure the evils in Crete, does not take Lycurgus's warning seriously. He believes Lycurgus is a wise man and therefore must also be master of his life or the "dueño de las estrellas" (vss. 1140–1179). Alarcón utilizes a very appropriate metaphor to express the relationship between the king and his new *privado*; the King is compared to a pen and Lycurgus to the hand that moves it (vss. 968–971). Lycurgus is willing to give advice as long as the King commands, but he makes it clear that he does not wish to take the sovereign's place. He has come only to point out the problems of Crete and to advise, but it is strictly the responsibility of the monarch to impose the remedies and to resolve its crisis (vss. 1130–1139). Olivares, to repeat, was a man who wished to be remembered as King Philip IV's humble servant and was, therefore, hesitant to take gifts from admirers for fear that the populace would think he was repeating the same self-interested behavior for which Lerma was denigrated. "Clean hands," as Elliottt observes, "would always remain an ideal of the Olivares administration..."[46]

Lycurgus ultimately accedes to the King's request and takes up the post. He is a man who obeys the will of the king, which he calls "justa ley" (vss. 467–469). God himself has ordered obedience to the king (vss. 980–983).

In Act II, at the end of Sc. 2, The King tells Lycurgus four policies which should be followed. These are reform policies which should be taken into account. First, he tells his *privado* not to feel intimidated and to feel free to tell him what changes need to be made. The king's relatives and servants should enjoy no special privileges, women's errors and weaknessness—especially if they are married—should be looked on with compassion, and magistrates should be severely punished if they commit crimes. The king is obviously aware of the desperate conditions of the nation and wishes to see improvements made.

In Act III, Sc.7, Lycurgus reads to the King the laws he has conceived to improve the economic, social, and moral state of Crete (i.e., Alarcón's Spain) and the King comments upon them. They are for the most part provisions echoing the reform proposals of Pérez de Herrera and not, of course, derived from the Spartan code. The figure of Lycurgus, the lawgiver in the play, reminds the audience that laws are vital to the strength and health of the public, but the laws proposed in the play respond to contemporary Spanish conditions. Such principles laid down by the historical Lycurgus as vesting legislative power equally in the congress and the king or enforced communal life (rather like that of a modern kibbutz) obviously find no echo in the play. Where there are similarities between the Spartan code and the play's proposed laws they lie in asking greater discipline from the citizenry and an increased devotion to the defense of the Empire.

Firstly, Lycurgus asserts that an edict should not be proclaimed until it has been well studied and considered. To have to revoke tomorrow the law you make today is a sign of imprudence and frivolity in a sovereign. The same sentiment is expressed in *Los favores del mundo* (vss. 2516–2517). Pérez de Herrera in his *Proverbios morales* similarly insisted that the number of *premáticas* be reduced but that those emitted should be strictly enforced. The first proposal is that young commoners, upon reaching their eighteenth year, give an account of the job that they hold in order to support themselves; and if they are found to be jobless, they should be forced to do public service (pp. 72–73). Noblemen who reach their twenty-fourth year without having served in the army for three years cannot enjoy the privilege of tax exemptions until they have done so (p. 73). When a rich man dies without children, he must leave to his consort, if she is poor, enough income to last her until she remarries (p. 73). The Junta de Reformación in 1623, at about the same time as the play, also attempted to aid poor women financially until they were married.[47] Michel Cavillac notes that there is a similar concern in *Guzmán de Alfarache*, and that Pérez de Herrera was probably the ultimate source of this concern for poor women.[48] Foreigners who wish to reside in the kingdom must be allowed to enjoy the same rights as heads of household and the native-born (p. 74). There is a *caveat* in the King's comment (vss. 2074–2077) when he says that he suspects that an abundance of foreigners is dangerous and may weaken a nation, but Lycurgus does not accept it. Instead he insists that foreigners become natives through friendship, commerce and residence because in time they too will have children and property acquired in their new country. This advice stems from the concerns and suggestions of Pérez de Herrera's propositions in his *Proverbios morales*, which encourage repopulation of the nation with more "useful" people, even if it means bringing back those who were at one time banished from Spain. It is possible that in the words of the ancient lawgiver, Alarcón was advocating permission for the Flemish and even the Portuguese Jews to enter the kingdom. As Alcalá-Zamora notes, the only persons permitted to aid in the colonization of America since the reign of Philip II were those of Spanish birth, the "naturales de los reinos."[49] All others of foreign birth were excluded from such a right. Alarcón, through Lycurgus, seems to protest such legislation as prejudicial and unjust. No doubt one of Alarcón's motivations was the fact that he was of Mexican birth. He was, more than other dramatists of his day, interested in the American empire:

> impresionó su ánimo juvenil la soledad de aquellos territorios inmensos, y cuando, al cabo de largo viaje, llega a la Metrópoli, le impresiona también la desolación de estos reinos, desangrados, sin fuerza demográfica para poblar rápidamente aquellas extensiones vastísimas. La solución la encuentra en la admisión de extranjeros, en la derogación de aquella ley, verdaderamente fundamental, dictada por Felipe II, mantenida por los sucesores; y previendo la resistencia de los monarcas austríacos y del Consejo, argumenta con tesón y valentía.[50]

Next, it is advised that magistrates not receive a fixed stipend from the royal treasury but that to each magistrate there should be given the stipend which corresponds to the quality of the office and the needs of the appointee (p. 74). Lastly, those who are denounced for crimes dangerous to the republic should not be exiled from where they were shamed but forced to live in this same place (p. 75).

The young King's old counselor, Severo, un *viejo grave*, strongly recommends that the King follow the advice of the Spartan lawgiver.

Once again, any moderately perspicacious spectator would surely recognize that behind the masks of the young King and the old counselor Severo we see the faces of the young King Philip IV (who came to the throne in 1621 at the age of sixteen) and his old counselor Baltasar de Zúñiga, uncle of the Count of Olivares. (As Elliott writes, it was the conspiracy of both Olivares and his uncle which gained power for the former, Olivares). [51] Alarcón's choice of the name "Severo" is also indicative of the old courtier Zúñiga's personality, whom Elliott describes as a man of "grave features."[52]

Intermingled with the political theme of the play, there is also, as in all plays, a love intrigue. The King passionately desires Diana, Severo's daughter, but is not willing to make a commitment of marriage to her. Unaware of this situation, Lycurgus also falls in love with her. Not only is his love for Diana complicated by the fact that both he and the King love the same woman, but he also knows that he must cleanse his honor by fighting a duel with Diana's brother, Teón. Marcela, a cousin of Diana's, adds to this witch's brew her own love for Lycurgus and consequent jealousy of Diana.

Obedience and loyalty to the sovereign is stressed throughout the play. Diana is shocked that the courtier Palante came to the aid of the King in his attempted seduction of her during the night while her father was searching for Lycurgus. Palante's only explanation is that obedience to the king is law (vss. 526–527). Once again the Bodinian doctrine with regard to unquestioning obedience to a king's will is voiced.

Obedience of servants to their masters is also hailed in the play. Lycurgus refuses to let the peasants take out their wrath on Teón's servant, who only obeyed his master's orders in attempting to carry off Coridón's wife. It would be unjust to kill an obedient servant for an offense which he has perpetrated out of loyalty to his master. Instead, since he has risked his life for his master, he should be rewarded (vss. 217–229). The justice of Lycurgus is unique in that it is tempered with mercy toward the servant who has not planned the offense but has acted out of loyalty to his master, a quality which Alarcón admired.

The character Diana is portrayed in the play as a strong and independent woman who resists the King's attempts to violate her. In a lengthy and emotional scene, with sword in hand to illustrate her resolve, she makes it very clear that she will not cede to the King's desires simply because he is king. Hers is not a case of disobedience to the sovereign, since she follows her instincts of *natural razón*, which, as she explains, does not permit love and lust to coexist in one man's heart. She states clearly that if he truly loves her, he must then honor her (vss. 558–577) and threatens to kill herself if he does not obey her wishes, calling him an ingrate, and a deceptive tyrant who is violently opposed to "las leyes naturales." As a king, she continues, he should be aware of justice and as a man, he should follow the "poderoso dictamen" of reason (vss. 683–785). In other words, as Bodin affirmed, even a king is subject to the rule of natural law which forbids the rape of a woman, and a subject does not owe him obedience if his commands go against it (see Ch.I, p. 5). It should also be noticed that her threat of suicide is a foreshadowing of the end of the play.

Severo decides to give his daughter's hand to Lycurgus, to which the King also agrees, and they are married. Lycurgus, portrayed as a typical seventeenth-century courtier who cannot be happy until he has avenged the offense committed by Teón, releases the latter from prison, where he has been kept for other offenses and, dressed as the peasant Lacón, fights a duel with him and kills him. The stern lawgiver Lycurgus is also a typical *galán* bound by the honor code of seventeenth-century Spain in a laughable manner; Alcalá-Zamora is perfectly justified in calling him an *inverosímil galán*.[53] Before the marriage is consummated, Lycurgus is sent by the King to defend Crete from Spartan attack. During his absence, the lustful King, having just heard that his royal fiancée from Athens has died and swept by passion again, enters Diana's room with the assistance of two servants. Palante is again the loyal servant who encourages the King to enjoy the pleasures of Diana (vss. 2425–2428), and the jealous Marcela agrees to open Diana's doors for the King to enter. Alarcón never allows these characters to be punished for having helped the sovereign in his attempted seduction of Diana. They are loyal servants who uphold the belief in obedience to the king regardless of his intentions. The King enters the room, pretending to be her husband.

Lycurgus bursts in with sword held high to kill the intruder, not knowing he is the King. But, once aware of the intruder's identity, Lycurgus proclaims that the wise man is always "dueño de las estrellas," no matter how much the stars may incline him otherwise (vss. 2677–2678). He remembers well the prediction that he will either kill a king or be killed by one. Faced with the dilemma—the imperative to kill the agressor against his honor and the imperative to hold the person of the king sacred—he rejects tyrannicide as a possibility and kills himself. A legitimate monarch (Bodin insisted) cannot be punished by his own subjects.[54] However, as a seventeenth-century courtier who is keenly attentive to his honor, as we have seen in the combat with Téon, Lycurgus cannot continue to live dishonored and thus must kill himself. With his death he saves himself from disgrace, but more importantly, his suicide can be considered as the ultimate act of Lycurgus's loyalty to the King, who can now be given the chance to redeem himself from his sin of lustful passion by marrying the widowed Diana. Lycurgus, on the other hand, cannot be condemned for having committed suicide since, as a pagan, he is not bound by Christian morality. The plays ends in a typically equitable fashion with the King's marriage to Diana, and all wrongs redressed. The *privado*'s sacrifice has secured the health of the kingdom by preserving the life of the King.

The spectator or reader, however, is left considerably dissatisfied with this selfish king who cannot control his passion for a young married woman. The monarch allows his lust to control his actions, giving little regard to his subjects, whom he abuses, even though, at the beginning of the play, he is portrayed as a conscientious ruler whose largest concern is to improve the decaying conditions of Crete. The lesson that must be learned is that there can be health in a society only when the king himself is virtuous, since the sovereign must be a model of uprightness for his subjects to follow. His *privado* must also be virtuous, since he is the king's closest friend and confidant. (Not everything in the play is consistent. Lycurgus himself is far from admirable in covering up Teón's death at his hands until after he has enjoyed the favors of his bride, Diana [vss. 2381–2392]). The health of the kingdom depends on wise counsel and prudent execution of the law, a task in which both sovereign and *privado* must collaborate—a fine lesson for the new King Philip and his *privado* Olivares if they were prepared to hear it.

3. La amistad castigada

The date of composition of *La amistad castigada* is given by Bruerton as 1621, the year of the death of Philip III and the beginning of the reign of Philip IV.

As in *El dueño de las estrellas*, we are again introduced to a self-centered king who allows his passion for a young woman to damage the body politic under his rule. He is not a paragon for his subjects to imitate, and his *privado* is as self-seeking and lacking in conscience as is his king. In this play, even more than in *El dueño de las estrellas*, the Court is filled with self-seeking people who do not seem to care about the health and future of their country. We are offered another portrait of a corrupt monarch whose lack of virtue has evil influence upon the entire state. His continued lack of regard for the law has become a danger to his subjects, who, finally, with the help of a group of nobles, decide to force the king to abdicate in favor of his brother-in-law.

The political beliefs of the dramatist are made manifest through a love-intrigue in which the upholder of justice is finally awarded the ultimate prize, the hand of the beautiful Aurora, whom everyone desires. By the use of this complicated love-intrigue Alarcón is able to convey his innermost beliefs concerning the nature of kingship, the relation of the king and his *privado*, and the relation of the king to the law.

The action of the play takes place in Sicily, probably in Syracuse, during the reign of Dionysius (367–356 B.C.); Plutarch is once again the source.[55] The play is not really a historical drama about life in Syracuse in the fourth century B.C., but about the problem of tyranny and how a people may respond to it at any time. Dionysius the Younger served as a classical example of tyranny as Lycurgus the Spartan had served as a classical example of a lawgiver in the *El dueño de las estrellas*. Alarcón chose to utilize the historical character of Dionysius, because he is remembered in history as a cruel tyrant. Dionysius was reared without discipline, and with no understanding of the duties of kingship and was thus eventually deprived of power and banished. Plutarch relates the story of Dionysius in this way: King Dion of Syracuse observed that the young Prince Dionysius was of unstable character and feared that he might attempt to usurp his power. He attributed these irregularities of the young Dionysius to his need of education. Therefore he sent for Plato to provide the young man with appropriate training. In actuality what was really bothering Dionysius was the fact that Dion enjoyed the wealth and power he coveted for himself. He schemed to rid the kingdom of its rightful king, forcing Dion onto a vessel bound for Italy. The citizens of Syracuse were outraged by this tyrannical action. Dionysius dismissed Plato, promising to recall Dion back to Syracuse, a vow he had no intention of keeping.[56]

Dion, however, continued to enjoy popularity among the people, which again sparked the jealousy of Dionysius. He accused his own sister, Theste, of being a traitor because she was married to one of her brother's enemies, Philoxenus. Her spirited response to her brother earned her the respect of the other citizens and even the admiration of Dionysius: " I assure you," she said, "that I would esteem it a higher honour to be called the wife of Philoxenus the exile, than the sister of Dionysius the tyrant."[57] Alarcón undoubtedly found this strong-minded woman to be an inspiration. The Alarconian heroine is as steadfast and articulate about her strength and virtue as Theste.

Dion raised forces made up of friends, statesmen and philosophers in order to attack Dionysius and win back his rightful rule of Syracuse. It was a small army of eight hundred men, but it was an army of perfect discipline and courage. The news of their arrival in Sicily reached the Syracusans, and five thousand more, although ill-equipped, courageously came to join Dion's forces. They marched into Syracuse without meeting a threat from Dionysius, who was at that time in Italy. The procession of Dion's army was regarded by the Syracusans as a sacred omen, the triumphant entry of liberty. Upon Dionysius's return, the armies engaged in battle, leaving Dionysius defeated and banished from Syracuse.[58]

In the first act of the play , Alarcón, who has chosen to begin the play with Dionysius at the helm, introduces the conflict of citizen allegiance. King Dionysius tells his counselor Filipo of conspiracies to reduce his power as king (vss. 29–40). [59] He is afraid he is losing public favor to his prudent and valorous brother-in-law, Dión, to whom, he states, he owes the Crown (vss. 40–72) and who is his *privado* when the play opens (vs. 193). History called Dionysius and his father Dionysius the Elder "tyrants" because they had converted the Sicilian democracy into a one-man hereditary rule. Dionysius explains this in the play:

> que supuesto que sabéis
> que no son [crueldades mías]
> las que el nombre de [tirano]
> me han adquirido en Sicilia,
> [sino haber mi padre y yo
> convertido en monarquía
> su república], adornando
> nuestras dos frentes altivas
> de su laurel, reprimiendo
> voluntades y osadías;
> si cuando borrar pretendo

nombre que así me fastidia,
ocasionara delitos,
despertando alevosías,
la falsa interpretación
que al nombre *tirano* aplican
de *cruel*, justificara
en sus lenguas mi malicia. (vss. 235–252); [emphasis added]

But the major problem is that the King is consumed by love for Aurora, Dión's daughter, whom he cannot ask to marry, since it has already been arranged that he marry a woman from Carthage. The King asks Filipo to help him remove Dión from the Court, giving him freedom to enjoy his daughter.

We already know that Dionysius is a tyrant, since he is so described in historical texts. The illegal assumption of the Crown by his father, who passed it on to his son, is referred to again in Act II, Sc. 8, by Dión:

en el reino sucedió,
que su padre, contra el fuero
de la libertad, primero
[tiranamente] ocupó...(vss. 1476–1479); [emphasis added]

The action of the play will also show how Dionysius acquires the name of "tyrant" in its second meaning, i.e., a cruel and unjust sovereign.

The new *privado,* Filipo, is a model of corruption who encourages Dionysius to live in accordance with his passions irrespective of his responsibilities as king. Dionysius, incited by Filipo, agrees that his passions take precedence over the well-being of his country. Together they plan to deceive Dión in order to gain access to the daughter (vss. 73–84).

In a later scene, Dión requests permission from the King to give the hand of Aurora to Policiano. Dionysius, however, concerned only for his own desires, refuses the request. He gives the excuse that the time is not right for a marriage to take place, since he is suspicious of conspiracies against him (vss. 151–156, 159–192). He asks Dión to help him to discover who the traitors are by pretending himself to be disaffected (vss. 228–234). Dionysius's plan for discovering the "conspiracy" is intelligent, but its purpose is not to secure the state but to remove the honorable Dión from his side and substitute for him the corrupt Filipo as his new *privado.* He tells Dión to begin to complain about the King to others he comes into contact with so that the conspirators may take the opportunity to speak up against him (vss. 193–219); the King does not, however, wish Dión to be an *agent provocateur* of plots (vss. 219–234), and Dión carefully follows this injunction.

In Act I, Sc.V, Dión prevents the disappointed Policiano from cursing the name of King Dionysius so that he does not have to tell the King that he is a possible suspect in the conspiracy. He does not wish to set traps for Policiano to fall into. Instead he chooses to counsel resistance against conspiracy, advising Policiano to be prudent and patient. Subjects, he says, have no right to question the will of their king. The loyal subject obeys the will of the king without protest (vss. 313–368).

The despicable King is not bothered that he manipulates the truth in order to cover up his plan to enjoy Aurora's charms. He is truly a Machiavellian monarch who believes that the end—his personal satisfaction and security—always justifies the means, but Dión, a loyal subject, cannot understand the King's reason for refusing to give the hand of Aurora to Policiano. He remains, however, an obedient courtier who views the will of the King as law (vss. 313–326). He assures the King that he is at his service and that he will attempt to discover the alleged traitors; the preservation of the King's life and the security of Sicily are the overriding *razón de estado* for him (vss. 278–287). This strong statement of Dión's gives the spectator and the reader the notion that Dión is a wise man, unlike the self-seeking King and his new *privado*.

The love-intrigue becomes increasingly more complicated as the play develops. Diana, sister of Ricardo, another of Aurora's suitors, complains that Policiano now wants to wed Aurora. She is upset since Policiano had given her his promise of marriage long before (vss. 465–476). Aurora tells her servant Camila of her love for Ricardo, even though she would marry Policiano if Dión should so decide (vss. 582–595). Next, as incredible as it may seem, Filipo also falls madly in love with Aurora when acting as the intercessor for the King (vss. 673–687).

Inspired by his passion for Aurora, Filipo commits his first act of treason against Dionysius. Hoping to win her favor, he reveals to Aurora that the King will not marry her since a marriage contract for him has already been arranged with a woman from Carthage. Filipo tells her that the King only wishes to dishonor her (vss. 748–765 and 775–777). Aurora falls in love with Filipo and would like him to declare himself

(Act II, Sc. 12). She directs several questions to Filipo which raise the issue of Dionysius's tyrannical comportment: "¿Así paga beneficios? / ¿Así asegura lealtades? / ¿Así obliga voluntades / y recompensa servicios? / ¿Así el nombre de *tirano* / quiere borrar? ¿Y así intenta / en el reino que violenta, / acreditarse de humano?" (vss. 796–803; emphasis added). Even a legitimate monarch becomes a tyrant when he puts personal passion above public good and repays faithful service with ingratitude (see Ch.I, p. 4), and in the case of Dionysius, whose claim to the Crown was flawed, resistance from the people can be expected unless the monarch's policies change.

It is interesting that Plutarch also mentions this aspect of ingratitude in his account of Dión. After he had saved Syracuse from the tyranical rule of Dionysius, the citizens later favored the rule of one of Dión's jealous opponents, who proved to be incompetent. The Syracusans then came begging to Dión for his help again. He was quick to forgive his countrymen and returned as their ruler because he believed that they had already paid heavily for their ingratitude.[60]

Filipo, on the other hand, suffers no remorse for his act of treason. The worst that could happen to him if the King were to find out what he had done would be death. This, however, is not so painful a punishment as losing all hope of ever gaining Aurora's affections would be for him. For, as he states, the one who dares to face death has nothing more to fear (vss. 872–879). He repeats a second time that he does not fear the King (vss. 1728–1731). He is a courtier totally lacking in the love, fear and obedience which, as Díez Borque suggests, "son los tres vínculos que unen al súbdito con su Rey."[61] Fear and respect for the king must be part of the concept of obedience to the king.[62] Filipo is presented in this play as a courtier who is the total opposite of a loyal and obedient subject of the king.

In Act II, King Dionysius makes an equally abhorrent confession. He too realizes and admits that his passion for Aurora may cause him to lose the Crown, yet he says he is unable to resist her and is therefore, ironically, victim and subject to his own tyrannical passion ("sujetarme veo / del *imperio tirano* del deseo," vss. 907–908; emphasis added). The King offers the excuse that he is no longer the man he used to be. He is so wounded by his love for Aurora that he can no longer see his responsibilities clearly (vss. 921–934). As a victim of the tyranny of love he has lost his wisdom, and to "un loco, / la ciencia y el valor importan poco" (vss. 936–938).

Diana, in the meantime, is desperate to win back the affections of her fiancé, Policiano. She feels she has no other recourse than to see the King in hopes that he will help her. She is right in coming to him, since he promises not to allow Policiano to wed Aurora. This is probably the only occasion when Dionysius appears to behave responsibly as a king. He is present to hear the problems of his subject and is ready to come to her aid. However, he possesses an ulterior motive—his own selfish love for Aurora. He doesn't want Policiano to marry Aurora, not because it is important to him that a man uphold his honor and keep his promise of marriage once it has been pledged, but because he doesn't want anyone else to enjoy her. In any case, Diana is awarded royal support.

Alarcón now adds another dimension to the play. It is as if the dramatist is flipping the coin to the other side. On the one side we are presented with the overbearing passion of Filipo and the King, which cause them to behave so irresponsibly. On the flipped side of the coin we are now introduced to an entirely different kind of man. We meet the upright courtier Ricardo, who, having already professed his love for Aurora, takes a giant leap away from self-interest and decides to place the interests of the King before his own. Ricardo discovers that Dionysius is also in love with Aurora. He is portrayed as a complete contrast to the King and his new *privado* Filipo. Instead of the selfishness of the King and Filipo, about which this play is centered, in Ricardo we see a subject attentive to his duties and responsibilities. Putting his own interests aside, he refuses any further contact with Aurora and will not ask for her hand in marriage.

The King's plan to seduce Aurora is made possible when Dión, in response to royal command, sets off for Carthage to bring the King's future bride back to Sicily. Before his departure, however, Filipo again displays his treacherous character. Out of total self-interest arising from his own passion for Aurora, Filipo warns Dión of the King's intention to dishonor Aurora (vss. 2348–2365). Not only does he betray Dionysius, but he also distorts the true meaning of friendship by lying when he says that he was bound to tell Dión the truth because of the friendship they share (vss. 2386–2388). The loyal Dión at this point can no longer support a king who will dishonor him so gravely as to violate his daughter. From this moment on Dión's purpose is to gather allies among the Syracuse nobility to kill the King.

Friendship is one of the themes of this play, and the other is that of law and justice. Ricardo not only exemplifies the ideal of obedience to his King, which Alarcón obviously holds in the highest esteem but is also the paragon of true friendship. When asked by Dión to come to his garden late that night, he trusts his friend and does not ask questions, for Dión conceals from him his plan to counteract the evil intentions of the King.

In Act III, Sc. 4, Dionysius requests that the servant Turpín help him with his plan of seducing Aurora by opening the gates of Dión's home. The conversation between the *gracioso* Turpín and Dionysius is a mixture of both comedy and satire. Turpín is used as a source of entertainment by the dramatist when he insinuates that it is possible that he too is of royal blood. He offers this ridiculous explanation: if his father had eaten the meat of a sheep which had once grazed upon the grass of a pasture where the body of a king, killed in battle and never recovered, had decomposed into the soil of the pasture, then that would make him royal since he is a direct product of his father:

> .... Comienzo
> a argüir. ¿No pudo ser
> que un rey muriese en la guerra,
> y que su cuerpo perdido
> fuese en tierra convertido
> en el campo; y que esta tierra,
> del sol y el agua dispuesta,
> en yerba se convirtiese,
> y que un carnero paciese
> esta yerba, y que, digesta
> con el calor, el carnero
> en carne la convirtiera,
> y que esta carne vendiera
> a mi padre el carnicero,
> y la comiese mi padre
> y en sustancia la volviese,
> y que esta sustancia fuese
> la que me engendró en mi madre?
> Pues ves aquí cómo yo,
> sin que a ti te haya ofendido,
> aquel rey puedo haber sido
> que en la batalla murió. (vss. 2183–2203)

Following this bit of comedy, Turpín, as spokesman for Alarcón, offers a caustic comment about royal ministers; may the king live forever, "más que un ministro cansado, / de quien tiene un desdichado / la futura sucesión" (vss. 2209–2211). It is important to note that Alarcón has given a dual function to this *gracioso* who is not only a source of comedy and entertainment but one of constructive criticism. Given the time of this play, it is possible that the dramatist was referring to the old guard of the Lerma regime, seemingly hanging on forever to power, while the new generation of ministers waited impatiently in the wings.

The King, with the help of Turpín and accompanied by Filipo, enters the garden of Aurora. He is surprised to be greeted with the angry swords of Dión, Policiano and Ricardo, who are quick to defend the honor of the young woman. Aurora shouts at them to stop fighting in an attempt to protect the King, regardless of his misguided intentions. Ricardo, now recognizing the sovereign, refuses to use the sword against him. Both Dión and Policiano, on the other hand, have decided to kill him. Policiano calls him not a king but a tyrant (vs. 2657), a cruel and vicious ruler. Dión, through whose offices, as we have been reminded often throughout the play, Dionysius was crowned king, calls him an ingrate and an abuser of the power entrusted to him (vss. 2658–2660).

Amazingly it is Aurora, who at the beginning of this dramatic last scene had threatened to kill the King to save her honor (vss.2632–2633), who now acts as his legal defender. Aurora does not wish any bodily harm to befall the King, yet, at the same time, she realizes that because of his ill-treatment of his subjects, the King, a traitor to his people, must be deprived of the right to rule. (Lauer explains that politics cannot be separated from ethics, and that kings reign only as long as they are just.)[63] We must, however, she says, treat him with respect and place him in high esteem since a king is still divine and sacred regardless of his tyrannical behavior. She argues that the law should decide the punishment:

> Si el cetro le diste vos,
> vos en cuanto a ser [tirano]
> del reino, le disculpáis,
> pues sois en eso el culpado.
> Y si ingrato os ha ofendido,
> [el castigo que al ingrato]
> [dé la ley, ejecutad]:

> Rey le hicistes; despojaldo[*sic*]
> del cetro, pues que tenéis
> los grandes de vuestra mano.
> Pierda el beneficio quien
> usa dél para agraviaros;
> no reine quien reina mal;...(vss. 2660–2672); [emphasis added]

The wholly unprincipled *privado* Filipo takes no sides; he will wait to see who wins. The nobles of Sicily band together, like an estates general in Bodin's treatise, and they jointly lodge complaints against a king who is a tyrant in both senses of the word. He is both an illegitimate sovereign and one who puts personal passion before the best interest of his subjects. They are all convinced by Aurora's legal argumentation and decide to exile Dionysius as punishment for his attempted crime. Dionysius admits his guilt, saying that it is true that he has acted with ingratitude and irresponsibility, and therefore is no longer worthy of the Crown:

> Nobles de Sicilia, puesto
> que [la ley al que es ingrato
> condena a que restituya
> el beneficio a las manos
> que liberales lo hicieron],
> y della observantes tanto
> guardalla en todo queréis,
> yo en todo también la guardo;
> y así a Dión restituyo
> la corona que él me ha dado,
> y el cetro renuncio en él;...(vss. 2742–2752);
> [emphasis added]

Dión, who was the *privado* at the beginning of the play, is now the newly designated King of Syracuse, and *rey justiciero*. He is quick to become the dispenser of justice. He rebukes the disloyal Filipo for having divulged the secret plan of Dionysius, and he is exiled; but the loyal Ricardo, who had put himself at the side of Dionysius, the anointed monarch, is praised by the new King for having been a model vassal and is rewarded with the hand of Aurora. Finally, the *gracioso* Turpín, who had admitted Dionysius to the garden, is pardoned and maintained in service : "...; que tanto / quien a su rey obedece, / aunque fuese por mi daño, / ha merecido conmigo." (vss. 2849–2852).

Although superficially, with its complicated love intrigue, its *gracioso,* and its threats of violence to maintain honor, *La amistad castigada* is cast in the mold of a *comedia de enredo* or even *de capa y espada,* the force and power of the drama lie in its daring political message and not in an amusing solution of a love intrigue. This is the only political play of Alarcón's that involves such severe treatment of a king. Alarcón obviously saw some validity in the political theories of Mariana, who advocates the punishment of even a legitimate monarch if he chooses to violate the rights of his subjects. Mariana boldly challenges the boundless authority of kings and defends the right of resistance to a tyrant. He makes it plain that subjects do have a right to depose or punish a tyrannical ruler, since man was given the right to choose his own ruler. Since it is man himself who decides upon a superior out of self-interest, he can then depose the king later if his self-interest commands it. Mariana is unequivocal on the question of the binding force of the law. The king is as subject to the law as are the citizens. Therefore, the laws of the state are greater than the laws of the sovereign. A legitimate ruler who allows himself to fall into tyranny must be stopped for the sake of the entire state. Such a monarch, however, can be deposed only by public authority (see above Ch.I, pp.8 –9).

But in truth, the doctrine of this play is not as radical as Mariana's. The fact that Dionysius's claim to the Crown was tenuous made it possible to deal with harsh punishment of a king. The rebellion of the nobles against Dionysius is acceptable in Alarcón's terms only because Dionysius (like his father before him) occupied the throne by usurpation in the first place and not through the right of hereditary succession. Alarcón cleverly arranged the historical source to suit his needs by selecting a historical tyrant to be the sovereign of the play and by making it clear from the start that Dionysius owes the Crown to Dión. Dionysius then proceeds to behave in the manner of a tyrant and seeks to dishonor Dión's daughter. It becomes the responsibility of the group of nobles to exile Dionysius who has trespassed against the law. In this banishment, Alarcón follows Plutarch's account, but the law punishing ingratitude is Alarcón's invention. The law must punish him for ingratitude (a clever and somewhat sophisticated way of achieving non-violent punishment— Alarcón flees from violent solutions). Alarcón has created a drama which still maintains, as in *El dueño de las estrellas,* the importance of obedience and loyalty to the king regardless of how misguided his intentions may be, but at the same time Alarcón offers Philip IV and his ministers a warning that the law can protect the subjects from a tyrant. His intention perhaps was to illustrate to the new administration what can happen if a king and his ministers decide to ignore their responsibilities to the people. The *privado* Filipo has not encouraged the King to behave in a manner befitting a monarch. Instead he has resorted to evil tactics in order to compete with the King for the same woman, and the end holds disastrous results for both the tyrant King and this self-interested *privado* who are both exiled. When both the *privado* and the king are evil, disaster will ensue. Alcalá-Zamora remarks sensibly that Alarcón stresses "la importancia de igualdad ante la ley," even when the person of the king is involved.[64] Alarcón insists that the king behave in a manner becoming a sovereign since his position is a "magno deber y extrema responsabilidad."[65]

The opposite situation is dramatized in *Los favores del mundo*, where Garci-Ruiz and Juan are portrayed as perfect *privado*(s). Garci-Ruiz forsakes his love for Anarda when he learns that both he and the Prince are in love with her. Juan is always close by the side of the Prince Henry to counsel and help in all state and personal matters. And in *El dueño de las estrellas*, the good *privado* removes himself from competition with the king for a lady's affection by killing himself. Good *privado*(s) maintain loyalty to the monarch while giving him at times unpleasant advice. The monarch frequently reforms himself and follows the path of honor and responsibility. The state as a whole then prospers. But if the *privado* is disloyal, scheming, and untrustworthy, the king and the state are at peril.

I repeat that Alarcón seems to have found some validity in the theories of Mariana, which teach that the commonwealth has the right to retract the grant of power and depose a king who has neglected to fulfill the office in a manner becoming a monarch. He may also have found it convincing that the king, according to Mariana, is not responsible to God alone but is also accountable to his people and to the laws of the land. Alarcón found validity in the political theories of both Bodin and Mariana. He clearly follows Bodinian thought when it comes to obedience to the king. As we recall, the servant Turpín is praised for his unswerving obedience to sovereign command even at the risk of Aurora's honor. Ricardo is awarded the hand of the desirable Aurora for his unselfish loyalty to King Dionysius. Bodin, like Mariana, makes the king responsible to his subjects, but he allows no act against a tyrannical monarch; he will answer to God and not to man. The unified opposition to a tyrant would be impossible in Bodinian terms. There are two reasons why Alarcón could allow the punishment of a king: 1) because Dionysius was not a legitimate monarch and 2) because historically he was actually banished. Alarcón seems quite daring in presenting so unfavorable an image of a king on the stage, especially when royal favor was an important factor in the success of a playwright. It is important to repeat, however, that Alarcón protects himself from censorship by portraying an historically oppressive tyrant, Dionysius, who holds the Crown "illegitimately."

4. Ganar amigos

Ganar amigos, whose composition is dated by Bruerton in the years 1620?–1622, was performed before the Queen in October, 1622.[66] It appears to be a historical play which takes place at the Court of Pedro I of Castile (1350–1369) in Seville but there is no attempt to create the atmosphere of a medieval court. Ballads and chronicles conferred upon Pedro the conflicting epithets of *Justiciero* and *Cruel*; this play emphasizes the epithet *Justiciero* (justice-dispenser). In his Court the *privado* and loyal citizens all cooperate in maintaining a model society in which the law is strictly but compassionately applied. In the words of doña Flor, which express the conviction of Alarcón, it is the king who must be the true dispenser of justice (vss. 607–610). [67]

It is also interesting to note that Pedro I had a close relationship with the city of Seville which Alarcón loved. Further, the wardenship of the Alcázar de Seville was a hereditary honor in the Olivares family, and on October 20, 1622, close to the time of the performance of this play, Philip IV named Count Olivares the perpetual warden of the Alcázar.[68] There is reason to believe that Pedro I and his *privado* Fadrique represent idealized portraits of Philip IV and Olivares. Among all the political plays of Alarcón, *Ganar amigos* is the only one in which both the sovereign and his *privado* are models of virtue. Particularly is this true in the case of the *privado,* who understands that the health of the community as a whole is based on trust, friendship, and a general regard for the law.

Alarcón may have also chosen Pedro I to be the king in this drama because he found certain similarities between his policies and those of Olivares. Like Olivares, Pedro I was hated by the landholding nobility since he wanted to work toward the restoration of economic stability by favoring the mercantile, city-dwelling bourgeoisie, which included the Jews. Olivares's proposals for economic revival were, in general, very similar. For example, he felt that the Sephardic Jews exiled in Portugal could help to improve economic conditions and chose to invite them back.[69]

In the first act of the play, the protagonist, the Marqués Don Fadrique, is introduced. There is a duel between don Fernando de Godoy, a one-time lover of doña Flor, and a stranger who attempts to draw him away from her window. The stranger is killed by Fernando, who then flees from the scene. As he runs, he meets up with the Marqués Don Fadrique, Pedro's *privado*, and desperately begs him for his protection, which the latter swears to give. Later, however, Fadrique feels hard-pressed to keep his word to protect Fernando when he discovers that the man killed by Fernando was his own brother. Fadrique, a man of honor, keeps his promise to protect Fernando and absolves him of guilt when he is questioned about the murder (vss. 330–332). Fernando is astounded by this act of mercy by the Marqués and believes that Fadrique has protected him now only to avenge himself in his own way later (vss. 339–342). In a following conversation, however, Fernando learns that Fadrique has pardoned him for no other reason except that he felt bound by the promise he had given to him earlier (vss. 377–387). Deeply wounded by the loss of his brother, the Marqués, nevertheless, is ultimately a man of his word. This lack of revengeful anger is almost a constant in Alarcón's theater and accounts in great part for the originality of this dramatist.

The complications of a love-triangle are soon introduced. Fernando, a past admirer of doña Flor, has given his word to Flor never to divulge this information to anyone for it would bring her honor into question. Fernando is bound by his promise of secrecy to Flor. But when the play opens, Fadrique is paying court to Flor and, as a concerned admirer, persists in questioning Fernando's reasons for being under her window the evening of his brother's death. Fernando, however, refuses to comment, holding fast to the promise he made to Flor (vss. 422–426). He views his promise to her as an obligation, just as Fadrique considered it his obligation to keep his word to protect Fernando from the authorities. Both men are therefore portrayed as honorable men whose first principle is to be true to their word.

Fadrique's love for Flor, however, reveals a flaw in his character, since he plans to enjoy Flor without offering her marriage. His servant Ricardo, however, advises him against this kind of behavior, unworthy of a royal *privado*.

Fernando later eases Fadrique's mind and tells him that he has not violated doña Flor's honor, only that he considers the secret between him and Flor "un inviolable sacramento" (vs. 849). Even after losing a duel to Fadrique, caused by his reluctance to disclose information about Flor, and threatened with death, Fernando does not yield (vss. 897–898). Fadrique is astounded by Fernando's valor and his steadfast adherence to his pledged word; theirs is a case of mutual admiration, since Fernando has not forgotten that the Marqués saved him from arrest by the authorities. This reminds us of the play *Los favores del mundo*, when Garci-Ruiz pardons the offender who invokes the Virgin for help. Twice Fadrique exemplifies the ideal of temperance. The Marqués does not turn Fernando over to the authorities for the death of his brother and pardons Fernando for his secrecy concerning Flor. Both Fadrique and Fernando pledge a lasting friendship to one another (vss. 931–934).

Later the King commands Fadrique to secretly kill don Pedro de Luna, who was caught in an illicit love affair with a lady living in the Court and thus under royal protection. Fadrique, however, finds it difficult to administer such a cruel sentence upon Pedro who he knows is a valiant and indispensable general of the army. To kill him would be a disservice to the country. Instead, he postpones executing the King's sentence and decides to take it upon himself, for the betterment of his country, to try to convince Pedro de Luna to leave the Court by offering him command of the troops in Granada. Fadrique uses his discretion and makes the decision that he feels will benefit the country most. Pedro de Luna, nevertheless, is envious of the close relationship between Fadrique and the King and renounces the offer vehemently, believing it a plan by Fadrique to rid himself of competition for the King's favor. Fadrique, however, realizes that the only way to save Pedro de Luna from death would be to persuade the King of his exceptional abilities as a general and to have the King order him to battle instead, which he does. Pedro de Luna goes to Granada, and the battle is won, for which the King thanks his *privado*. Fadrique explains that it was not disobedience or resistance which urged him to go against the King's will, but prudence. The rigor of the law, he explains, must at certain times yield to the higher principle of reason of state (vss. 1921–1932).

Clearly, Alarcón approves of the *privado* who, with prudence, attempts to dissuade his sovereign from rash policies. Blind and injudicious obedience to the king, therefore, is not advocated by Alarcón (nor was it by Bodin—see Ch.I, p. 5), who recommends the use of prudent judgment when the well-being of the nation is at stake. This decision by Fadrique to spare the life of an indispensable soldier reflects the concern of Alarcón about the weakening conditions of the national defense. (It was also a proposal of Pérez de Herrera to reduce the number of holders of useless occupations [notaries, etc.] by converting these people into soldiers, traders, artisans, farmers, and cattle raisers. Later the Junta under Olivares proposed to abolish the taxes on domestic goods in order to give more money to soldiers in hopes of attracting more able men to improve the national defense.)

The love plot becomes even more complicated when Doña Ana, a friend of Flor's, decides to intercede for the sake of Flor's interests. Because of the shadows of doubt cast on Flor's honor, Fadrique has stayed away from her. When Ana speaks to Fadrique on Flor's behalf, Don Diego de Padilla, brother of Flor, who is in love with Ana, misinterprets their conversation, believing that Fadrique and Ana are lovers, and consequently plans revenge on the Marqués. He enters the room of Ana, identifying himself as the Marqués, and violates the helpless woman.

After the rape, Doña Ana realizes that the only person who can help her to avenge this criminal act by (as she mistakenly believes) Fadrique, is the King. She is right in her conviction, because he is quick to apply justice even to his most valued counselor. The King tells Ana: "En mi justicia / no hay excepción de persona" (vss. 2119–2120). He immediately enforces the law by imprisoning Fadrique and condemning him to death. One can only imagine the hardship suffered by the King when compelled to sentence the *privado* who has become his most trusted friend. King Pedro, as *rey justiciero*, however, disregards personal sentiments and shows "unshakable attachment to justice."[70] He knows that justice must be administered impartially if his country is to remain a healthy body politic in which all men are equal under the law. As Maravall suggests, the Council of Trent, which first met in 1545, proclaimed the equality of all men with respect to grace, and this idea was then reflected in politics, which consequently stressed the equality of all men under the law.[71] The equality under the law of all citizens, as has been said, is frequently upheld in the plays of Alarcón, and what better person than Pedro I, "El Justiciero," to be the administrator of this nonpartial justice. Alcalá-Zamora has aptly described the responsibility of the king when he says: "La justicia es el principal atributo, la mayor preocupación, el esencial deber, la razón de existencia del poder real."[72]

Still, in this case, it would be a dreadful miscarriage of justice for the Marqués to be blamed for a crime which he never committed. Alarcón therefore cleverly devised a plan for the Marqués's release which would also highlight the courage and the virtue which the other courtiers have learned from the example set by the Marqués. Fadrique has always been a friend to all, and now others must, in turn, prove their friendship to him. Don Fernando persuades don Diego to confess before the King to the rape of Ana (Act III, Sc. 15). Likewise Fernando confesses to the murder of Fadrique's brother, of which crime many falsely accused Fadrique, and finally Don Pedro de Luna realizes that Fadrique wanted him to fight in Granada not because he wished to be rid of competition for royal favor, but to save him from execution. He nobly offers to change places in prison with the fallen *privado*, an offer which Fadrique rejects. Thus, "the court is cleansed of mean deceits and petty jealousies as the result of the noble example of the Marquis— and to a lesser degree Fernando—which has rekindled in all these courtiers an awareness of the obligations of noblilty, not the least of which is keeping one's word to a friend."[73]

In the play, Alarcón criticizes envy because it is the root of much evil. It is the envy which Diego feels toward the Marquis, because he thinks Ana loves him, which causes Fadrique's fall from royal favor. Envy is also the root of even further malicious remarks by Fadrique's enemies, who, like Pedro de Luna, are jealous of his privileged position. They slander his name by accusing him of murdering his own brother, who was also in love with Flor.

Friendship, however, acts as a contrast to envy in the play. There is a strong bond of friendship established between Fadrique and Fernando in the beginning of the play, and this bond is partly responsible for saving Fadrique's life in the end. Pedro de Luna and don Diego at the close of the drama also realize the importance of friendship and, placing themselves in jeopardy under the law, they come to the aid of a friend, the Marqués. There is also a strong bond of friendship between the King and his *privado* which the King values highly (vss. 1949–1950); but as the principal executor of justice, he cannot allow friendship to interfere with the impartial application of the law. In *Ganar amigos* it is suggested that although there is a close tie established between king and *privado*, there can be no favoritism shown toward the *privado* when he commits an infraction of justice. The force of the law must be equally binding for ministers and subjects alike.

Obedience to the king and to reason are other issues which should be examined. It is important to emphasize again the occasion when Fadrique deliberately goes against the will of the King, who wanted don Pedro killed for having transgressed the laws of the Court. Fadrique does not give blind obedience to his sovereign. On the contrary, Fadrique saves Pedro's life for the sake and advantage of the entire nation. The anonymous author of the *Estrella de Sevilla* perhaps shared the same beliefs as Alarcón but chose to present his views differently. The protagonist in this play is the courtier don Sancho, who tragically kills his friend and future brother-in-law, Busto Tavera, at the request of the monarch, who has been caught by the latter trying to seduce his sister. Because of the extremity of the situation in which Sancho is forced to kill his best friend and future brother-in-law, it seems convincing that this playwright disapproved of blind obedience to the king. The audience and reader are left with a feeling of total indignation at the injustice of the situation. Alarcón, on the other hand, suggests a critical attitude toward mechanical obedience to the king in another way. His protagonist utilizes his gift of reason in order to persuade the King to change his mind for the sake of the entire nation. Discretion, which Alcalá-Zamora points out to be one of Alarcón's obsessions, is certainly utilized by this prudent *privado* for the benefit of the state.[74]

Similarly King Pedro uses his God-given gift of reason. He has been a steadfast champion of the law throughout the play, but at the close he surprises the spectator and pardons all the courtiers of their offences, including don Diego, the rapist, and don Fernando, the murderer. He does so following a (fictitious) provision of the legal code of Castile which grants pardon on one occasion to those people who are, like don Pedro, beneficial to the nation as a whole, "que el derecho prevenido / más conveniente juzgó / conservar el bien de muchos / que castigar un error" (vss. 2829–2832). These men, as well as Fadrique, are therefore pardoned by the King in accordance with the law (vss. 2842–2844). (So it was in *La amistad castigada* that a way is found through the *law* to depose a tyrant.) Fadrique, who once advised the King that it is not always best to impose the strictest law to the detriment of the entire state, has thus benefitted by his own counsel. Don Fadrique, don Fernando, don Diego, and don Pedro de Luna have proven that their valor is worthy of pardon and that they are an asset to the entire community. Through the force of the law and justice these men are all pardoned and receive their liberty; "justice" in the highest sense will find in the law provisions for clemency and pardon. The King gives the hand of Ana to Diego, since it was he who violated her honor, and he allows Flor to choose her husband (vss. 2850–2851). As in *Los favores del mundo*, Flor is a decisive woman who will not allow others to decide her future. She, of course, selects Fadrique to be her husband, since she has loved him from the beginning of the play. Alarcón again stresses the freedom of choice for women when he gives doña Flor the opportunity to elect her own husband.

Alarcón's view of the relationship of the king to the law is never clearly stated, but in the third act his philosophy is hinted at briefly in a conversation between don Diego and the *gracioso* Encinas. Diego, in a typically Bodinian comment, says that there is no law which binds the king since he is author of all laws (vss. 2226–2228). Encinas replies that once the king has publicly announced his decree, he too is then bound by such a law (vss. 2229–2232). Encinas appears to be following the theory of Mariana, which suggests that the law binds even the king who has made it.

Encinas also acts as spokesman for Alarcón in another circumstance. Portrayed as a noble character who refuses to betray his master even when money is offered as a bribe, he comes to the aid of all servants in general by speaking out in defense of their honor and virtue, since they are most usually condemned as avaricious and cowardly (vss. 2245–2264). Alcalá-Zamora refers to this scene of the play as another important expression of "la esencial igualdad humana" which is frequently evidenced in Alarconian plays.[75]

Another important factor to remember, since here lies much of Alarcón political beliefs, is that in this play there is a special emphasis placed on limiting the severity of punishment. This policy is adapted by

Fadrique, who is merciful toward don Fernando at the beginning of the play, and again shows compassion toward don Pedro de Luna later on. The King, having learned this policy from his *privado*, also practices this policy of justice tempered by mercy when he forgives all wrongs at the end of the play. Fadrique, who has been the epitome of clemency, finally profits from the policy of clemency he has recommended to the King. *Ganar amigos* is a play that portrays a model Court where "even servants and women behave with honor, earn respect, and are protected."[76] And the person responsible for the uprightness of the kingdom is the King's *privado*, don Fadrique, who has always upheld the belief that mercy, when the law permits it, is the best policy.

Ganar amigos sets before the new King Philip and his *privado* Olivares the qualities of a model government. Since the play was performed at the Court by the company of Alonso de Olmedo in October 1622, in all probability, Olivares was there to witness its performance. Olivares would have been pleased to see such an ideal administration inspired by so noble a character as Fadrique, upon whom everything depends. It may be plausibly conjectured that Olivares found *Ganar amigos* to be a very "suitable drama for the education of his monarch and the exaltation of himself as *privado*."[77]

5. Los pechos privilegiados

Los pechos privilegiados was composed, according to Bruerton, sometime between 1620?–1625? And, despite its harsh criticism of egotistical monarchs, the play was performed at the Court in 1625 and 1627. The praise of the Villagómez name in this play, however, may be motivated by Alarcón's desire to please a counselor of the Indies from 1621 until 1642 named Pedro de Vivanco y Villagómez.[78] The play begins at the Court in León but later alternates between the countryside of Valmadrigal and the Court. Two kings are introduced in this play: Alfonso V, King of Asturias and León (994–1027), and Sancho Garcés III of Navarra (1000–1035). These kings are historical characters, as are Melendo González, Count of Galicia, and his wife Doña Mayor, who, as Mariana indicates in his *Historia general de España*, were called to Court to become royal tutors to the young Alfonso V. King Alfonso later married doña Elvira, daughter of Count Melendo;[79] this historical background once again was drawn from Mariana's *Historia*.[80] Alarcón portrays these two kings with contrasting characters. King Sancho is described as an upright and responsible monarch while Alfonso is portrayed as a lustful king, insensitive to his duties to his subjects. The remaining characters, on the other hand, are the creation of the imagination of the dramatist.[81] The protagonist, Rodrigo de Villagómez, a fictitious ancestor of the prominent Villagómez family and, at the beginning of the play, the *privado* of King Alfonso, is described as a man of courage and honor and of a very illustrious family background (vss. 651–652 and vs. 1268). [82]

The drama begins when King Alfonso orders his *privado* Rodrigo to help him devise a plan by which he will be able to enjoy the charms of Elvira, daughter of Count Melendo, a retired *privado* and tutor of the young king. He asks him to act as intermediary for him. His intentions are wholly dishonorable, since he has already planned to marry the Infanta doña Mayor, a princess of Castile. Rodrigo, however, refuses to obey the King and advises him to marry Elvira instead of dishonoring her. Rodrigo feels bound not only by the special friendship which he and Count Melendo share but also obliged by justice, which he places before his own personal ambition as *privado* to the King. He is offended and shocked that Alfonso could possibly request such an ugly favor of him (vss. 213–228). Rodrigo explains to the King that true friendship does not mean blind obedience to a king's wishes; rather it should prompt good advice (vss. 172–176). Nor does the *law* accept the excuse of friendship as justification for a crime (vss. 185–186). Honor, in Rodrigo's opinion, is not something which should be sacrificed in order to attain such ambitious goals as the post of *privado* to the king. Rodrigo offers a criticism of the contemporary situation at Court, where it is a common practice for men to give up their honor and dignity in order to climb the ladder of success (vss. 237–248). Merit, he says, should serve as the only indication of a man's ability to serve as *privado*; flattery of the king and condonation of his vile acts do the monarch no service (vss. 246–249). There are many men, Rodrigo says, who would be willing to lose their honor for ambition's sake (vss. 265–268), but he adds that, unlike the others, he would prefer to lose his position at Court rather than to compromise his integrity. The King dismisses Rodrigo from his post but commands him not to divulge his passion for Elvira to anyone.

In a powerful soliloquy, Rodrigo denounces ambition to rise to splendid heights at Court when it means the loss of honor and dignity. It is interesting to note that both the King and Rodrigo use the phrase "nunca mucho costó poco" (vss. 292 and 332), but the two men have separate interpretations. For the misguided sovereign, the "mucho" means the high position at Court where honor and dignity may be lost if ambitious desires are to be fulfilled. On the other hand, for Rodrigo, "mucho" means virtue. One cannot maintain both honor and high positions at Court simultaneously, and if given the choice, Rodrigo would choose to protect his honor even if it means the loss of his position at Court. Rodrigo not only elects to maintain his honor but also chooses to uphold the obligations imposed by his friendship with Count Melendo. Rodrigo is strong in his conviction; his only regret upon leaving the Court is that he also forgoes the chance to marry the woman he loves, Leonor, the other daughter of Count Melendo.

Ramiro becomes the successor to Rodrigo. The *gracioso*, Cuaresma, tells him that he can be either a *privado puro*, who indulges the king's every desire and therefore runs the risk of criticism from others, or he can be a *privado aguado*, whose responsibility it is to govern the country properly. The *gracioso,* however, compares the latter position to the eternal misery of hell itself:

> Va la explicación. Aquel
> que tratando el Rey con él
> sólo las cosas que son
>   de gusto, vive seguro
> de quejosos maldicientes
> y cansados pretendientes,
> llamo yo [privado puro];
>   mas [*sic*] el triste a quien le dan
> un trabajo tan eterno,
> que es del peso del gobierno
> un lustroso ganapán
>   (aunque al poeta desmienta
> que suele llamallo Atlante
> pues no hay cosa más distante
> del cielo que éste sustenta,
>   que la carga del gobierno,
> que infierno se ha de llamar,
> si es que el eterno penar
> se puede llamar infierno);
>   éste, pues, que siempre lidia
> con tantos, tan diferentes
> cuidados, que a los prudentes
> da compasión, y no envidia;

éste, que no hay desdichado
caso, aunque sin culpa suya,
que el vulgo no le atribuya,
llamo yo [privado aguado];... (vss. 338–364);
[emphasis added]

One can surely see the sympathy for the King's chief minister here in these lines. The dramatist utilizes words of the *gracioso* in order to make it clear that the task of *privado* is not an easy one, especially if he is to be of genuine service to his king and his country. He is implying that if the job is to be done properly, then frustration and heartache must necessarily follow. Ramiro chooses to be a *privado puro*, since he believes that the wishes of the King are law and must, therefore, be obeyed. Cuaresma warns him that the *privado* is always blamed by the people when things go wrong (vss. 394–399), but Ramiro, headstrong in his attempt to gain power and wealth, decides that he will exert every effort to gain Elvira for the King.

When approached by Ramiro, Elvira is quick to defend her honor. She is willing to mary King Alfonso, but she will not permit him to dishonor her (vss. 453–460). Like other Alarconian women examined in this study, Elvira is portrayed as a strong-willed woman who makes it clear from the start that she will do all in her power to protect her self-respect and honor. Rodrigo, the fallen *privado*, bids farewell to Leonor before he departs for the town of Valmadrigal, where he decides to go in order to escape the King's displeasure and to avoid the embarrassment and harassment at Court. He does not give any explanation for his departure, since he feels obliged by the promise of secrecy he gave to the King. It is difficult for Rodrigo to leave his friend, Count Melendo, without explanation and without Leonor as his wife. Count Melendo attributes Rodrigo's withdrawal from Court to the fact that perhaps the King is also in love with Leonor. He admires such an honorable man of the Villagómez family who would never compete with the King for the same woman's affections.

Both Count Melendo and his son Bermudo, attentive to their family honor, become suspicious of Ramiro's intentions. Melendo is no fool and has now figured out that Ramiro is a traitor who has earned his *privanza* by acting as the King's go-between with Leonor (it will be some time before he discerns that Elvira is the daughter being coveted). The Count questions the credibility of the justice of the court system where honor and dignity are given to those who indulge the King's desires (vss. 705–708).

Nuño, the servant of Count Melendo, proves his loyalty to his master when he confesses to having consented to open the doors of the house that night for Ramiro to enter and see Elvira. He explains that he did so out of fear of revenge (vss. 734–740). This confession is responsible for helping to conserve Elvira's honor. The Count is appreciative of his servant's honesty and refers to him now as his friend rather than servant (vss. 749–752).

The Count now asks for forgiveness for suspecting the King of attempting to dishonor his daughter Leonor. To presume guilt of a king, a *sacra persona*, as he refers to Alfonso, is quite an extreme accusation since, as he explains, in Bodinian terms, the king is the life of the law and the soul of justice:

> (*Ap*. Perdona,
> Rey, si tu sacra persona
> injustamente culpé:
>   error fue, que no malicia,
> presumir culpa de un rey
> que es la vida de la ley
> y el alma de la justicia.) (vss. 767–772)

Knowing what we know, this statement is heavily ironic in this situation. In his apology, what is stressed is the monarch's responsibility to behave justly, and that is not this King's intention. We are again reminded of Lauer's words that politics and ethics cannot be separated, and that a king can reign only as long as he is just.[83]

The night comes when Ramiro and the King enter the house of the Count with Nuño's help. The Count and his son are, however, hiding nearby. Elvira is shocked upon seeing the King, who threatens to kill her father if she screams for him. The Count and his son, however, appear to protect Elvira from the intruder. Upon recognizing Alfonso, however, the Count drops his sword immediately. He is unable to draw his sword against this sacred person. This rejection of violence on the part of Melendo toward the King again adheres to the philosophy of Bodin, which does not permit active resistance against the person of the king. He does, however, reproach his sovereign in the strongest terms, reminding him that he should esteem his reputation as a just king more than life itself (vss. 873–880). The King attempts to lessen his guilt by blaming *ciego amor* for his vile behavior and promises to desist from his suit, convinced by the strong words of his former *privado*.

Alarcón is able to determine the punishment of the King in a clever and equitable manner. Since the crime was never consummated, the King insists that the punishment should fit only the intention of crime. Had any other man attempted to rape the Count's daughter, death would have been the only suitable punishment. This case, however, is quite different since it is the King who is the offender. Alfonso suggests that the only appropriate punishment for him would be the vituperation which he has already received from Melendo; to this the Count agrees.

Melendo is unaware that the King will again attempt the same crime. He is convinced that the sovereign has learned his lesson, since he has already been warned. Mariana had advised (see above, Ch.I, p. 9) that a legitimate monarch must first be warned and given the opportunity to change his evil ways. If, however, he does not heed the warning, it is admissible for the commonwealth to retract the grant of power from the king. King Alfonso has been given fair warning about his vicious behavior but his conversion to virtue will be short-lived.

The Count, moved by his friendship with Rodrigo, goes to the King on Rodrigo's behalf, requesting that the King permit his return and to allow Rodrigo and Leonor to marry, though Rodrigo has firmly told him he will not return to his position as *privado*. To do so would be as foolish as for Phaethon, having once survived the trip in the sun's chariot, to ask to drive it again (vss. 989–1003). It is not only that the *privado* is forced to take the blame for any wrong-doing of the sovereign, but the worst is that he must make the choice either to indulge the king and his desires in order to maintain his position, or, as is the case of Rodrigo, take the chance of being dismissed from his position because he has followed his conscience and has not conspired with the king to commit an action which he knows in his heart is wrong. This attention to morality frequently surfaces in the plays of Alarcón, and with Rodrigo's dilemma, Alarcón's insistence upon virtue and good conscience becomes very apparent. Tierno Galván's statement seems to hold true at least with regard to Alarcón: "Para los pensadores políticos españoles del Siglo de Oro, la política es sierva de la moral, según la cosmovisión católica."[84]

Ramiro promises, as would be expected, to help the King in his second attempt to enjoy Elvira. In return the King consents to give the hand of Leonor, whom Ramiro loves, to him instead of to Rodrigo. Alarcón has again utilized a woman as the reward for just behavior. At this point in the play, the spectator and reader are not quite sure how this problem is to be resolved. Will the reward go to the obedient *privado*, no matter how debased his intentions, or to the upright man who refuses to obey the evil commands of the King?

King Alfonso, as he explains to Ramiro, prefers to reward the *privado* who is willing to put his conscience aside in favor of indulging the King, no matter how corrupt his intentions are. He tells Ramiro that he intends to give Leonor to him because he has loyally supported him in his quest to seduce Elvira, while he refuses the hand of Leonor to Rodrigo, since this latter *privado* places the law and good conscience before the desires of the King (vss. 1101–1118).

Count Melendo, realizing that the King is still intent upon dishonoring Elvira, is again confronted with the problem of a tyrannical king. Does he remain in León and resist the King actively and perhaps even kill him, or does he permit the King to have his way with his daughter? The answer for the Count is to flee from the King, since he believes that there is no other form of defense possible (vs. 1130). The Count explains to his son:

> El remedio está en la ausencia;
> que al furor de un rey, Bermudo,
> la espalda ha de ser escudo,
> y la fuga resistencia. (vss. 1143–1146)

Alarcón is again expressing his philosophy concerning what to do in a circumstance similar to the Count's when one's honor is threatened by a wayward king. The situation of a misguided sovereign who deliberately attempts to take advantage of his position by dishonoring a young woman is central to the plot of this play as it is in *El dueño de las estrellas* and *La amistad castigada*. The solution here offered is flight, thus removing the temptation and avoiding an all-out confrontation. Bermudo, the Count's son, agrees to leave the Court in León with his entire family for the town of Valmadrigal where, although he will be leaving prestige behind, he will be maintaining his family honor. He and his father also plan later to go to Galicia, renouncing their citizenship in León and the homage sworn to Alfonso of León (vss. 1147–1158). Alarcón has carefully planned the drama so that a solution to this problem can be worked out. In the opening scene at Valmadrigal, the peasants are singing a song welcoming those who have come there for solace. Alarcón contrasts the peace and tranquility of the countryside where one comes to rest with the toils and tribulations of city life.

Here we are introduced to King Sancho of Navarra, who has come to ask Rodrigo if he would intercede on his behalf with Count Melendo, since he wishes to marry Elvira. He also offers Rodrigo honor and estates in Navarra. The inclusion of a second king in the play is a clever ruse on Alarcón's part. The upright Don Sancho provides a telling contrast to the spoiled character of Alfonso, and serves in the long run to persuade King Alfonso to marry and not dishonor Elvira.

Meanwhile, the King of León asks his *privado* Ramiro for advice. Is it not better that he break "la fe y palabra real" than to die from love? (vss. 1488–1490). Ramiro, acting as *privado puro*, obliges the King by telling him that the laws are as flexible as wax in the hands of the king, and that a king can either make or break a law according to his design (vss. 1509–1515). Anything, in Ramiro's opinion, is acceptable to cure a heartsick monarch (vss. 1590–1591). Obedience and loyalty to the king are always applauded by Alarcón, but in this circumstance, he seems to be actually satirizing blind obedience to a king who lacks concern for the well-being of his nation, and who no longer considers it his responsibility to protect his subjects. He is also criticizing the ambition of ministers who stop at nothing to get ahead even if it leads to the dishonor of an innocent victim. And what about the victims, are they to accept the abuse without retaliation?

King Alfonso is infuriated when he discovers that the Count has left for Valmadrigal with his daughters and decides to follow them. His anger increases when he overhears a conversation between Rodrigo and Elvira and misinterprets it to mean that Rodrigo is in fact in love with Elvira, thus confirming what Ramiro had previously told him. The King and Ramiro draw their swords to kill Rodrigo, who defends himself, though he refuses to fight against the King. Rodrigo has remained loyal and has offered no resistance against his sovereign. The rustic wetnurse of Rodrigo, Jimena, appears, it seems from nowhere, to remove the King physically and forcibly from such a precarious situation. This action of Jimena's is wholly unlikely, but once again we see that active resistance or rebellion against a king is prevented. The character Jimena, as unconvincing as she is, and as Walter Poesse aptly suggests, "not a little ridiculous," [85] is able to carry the King off against his will. Her presence, however, is indispensable for Alarcón's purposes, since she illustrates his firm conviction that a sovereign should not be subject to violent attacks.

This scene undoubtedly inspired laughter at Court and still today invokes at least a chuckle from readers of Golden Age dramas. Jimena is an original creation of Alarcón who exemplifies the dramatist's dual purpose of entertainment and instruction.

In the final act, all conflicts are resolved. Villagómez defends Ramiro against the outraged villagers, thereby converting Ramiro to virtue by his brave and noble example (Act III, Scenes 2 and 4). For the one time in Alarcón's political plays, public opinion becomes a major check on royal power. It is because of public opinion that King Alfonso restores Rodrigo to power. He tells Ramiro that he must reinstate Rodrigo as his *privado* because the people of León are complaining about his dismissal:

> ....León
> contra mí, según he sido
> informado, da atrevido
> rienda a la murmuración;
>   que en mi gracia lleva mal
> de Rodrigo la mudanza,
> que por sus partes alcanza
> aplauso tan general. (vss. 2252–2259)

Public opinion, as a restraint on monarchical power, is again emphasized when the King states:

> Al fin, es forzosa ley,
> por conservar la opinión,
> vencer de su corazón
> los sentimientos el Rey. (vss. 2312–2315)

The King therefore asks Rodrigo to serve again as his *privado*, but Rodrigo refuses, preferring to remain on his country estate (Act III, Sc. 12). A similar sentiment can be found in *Los favores del mundo* when Garci-Ruiz says he would choose to remain in the country, away from the toils and frustration of court life.

When Alfonso learns that Elvira is to wed don Sancho of Navarre, he attempts to sequester her but is stopped by don Sancho, who is also a king, and in Valmadrigal they are equal antagonists. Count Melendo, who sees the two kings fighting, draws his sword to take the side of don Sancho, since he has renounced his oath of fealty to Alfonso and gives his loyalty to Sancho of Navarre (vss. 2354–2359). Rodrigo, however, moved by loyalty to Alfonso, valiantly defends the King against his own two friends, Melendo and King Sancho. Loyalty to the king, he says, must always take precedence over friendship (vss. 2753–2756). Jimena again miraculously appears to protect Alfonso by drawing a sword against don Sancho and the Count. Elvira, portrayed as a woman of strength and character, speaks her own mind to King Alfonso. As spokesman for the dramatist, Elvira—like Aurora in *La amistad castigada*— intervenes, saying that the King's perverse behavior has offended the principles of both God and man: "¡el suelo y el cielo ofendes!" As both a Christian and a king, he must rectify the situation. His quarrel, she adds, is not with don Sancho or the Count, but with her, since *she* will give her hand to Sancho rather than suffering the dishonor of being Alfonso's mistress. She tells him, in no uncertain terms, that he must marry her, or she will wed don Sancho, King of Navarre (vss. 2771–2801). He finally yields to his love for her and asks her to marry him. King Alfonso pardons Count Melendo, and the hand of Leonor is given to Rodrigo; Ramiro, now Villagómez's friend, puts up no resistance. Ramiro is not punished because, although his intentions to aid in the seduction of Elvira are less than admirable, he was, nevertheless, obeying the King's wishes and wholly supports Villagómez's restoration in the King's grace. Alfonso honors the loyal Jimena, the wetnurse of the valiant Villagómez's and the King's protection, by raising her to hidalgo status.

In the end, the virtue of two *privado*(s) (Rodrigo and Melendo) produces the return of King Alfonso to proper behavior. It is important to remember that, throughout the play, nobody defies the King physically (except Melendo after he has renounced allegiance to him). On the contrary, Alfonso's subjects remain loyal to him unless their integrity is threatened by him, in which case they simply flee from his presence. But the nobility of the *privado*'s example slowly but surely restores the King's sense of propriety, just as earlier Villagómez's defense of Ramiro against the outraged villagers has brought Ramiro back to the path of virtue. Order is restored in the state once the King has learned that to maintain his reputation among his vassals he must curb his violent and destructive caprices (vss. 2312–2315).

B. Plays about Revolts against Legitimate Monarchs

Two other plays, *La crueldad por el honor* and *No hay mal que por bien no venga*, deal with attempted treason against legitimate monarchs. The problem of the relation of the legitimate monarch or the usurper to a *privado* is also treated, but this relationship is not the focus of dramatic interest as in the five plays discussed above. It should come as no surprise that both of these plays proclaim once again the inviolability of a legitimately held crown.

1. La crueldad por el honor

For *La crueldad por el honor* Alarcón once again chose Mariana's *Historia general de España* (Libro XI, capítulo ix) as the source for some historical facts in the play. In the year 1134, the King of Aragón, Alfonso I, disappeared after a battle in which the Moors defeated the Spanish. Rumors have it that he went to live in Jerusalem in order to escape from the life he was tired of living and to avoid the shame of having lost the battle. Since don Alfonso had no heirs, his brother Ramiro reluctantly assumed the throne. Ramiro was hesitant since he preferred the monastic life which he had chosen nearly forty years before, and he had been elected Bishop of Roda and Barbastro. His daughter, Petronila, married Count Ramón Berenguer, and she bore one son in the year 1152, who later ascended the throne as Alfonso II in 1162 when his mother turned over power to him. An impostor appeared two years before the young prince acceded to the throne claiming to be the long-vanished Alfonso I. There was an uncanny resemblance between the impostor and the monarch, who had disappeared twenty-eight years earlier. Such a long time lapse also impeded the clear memory of the king's features, but because of his general physical likeness and the nobles' "dissatisfaction" with the rule of a woman after Ramón Berenguer's death, the impostor was able to talk his way into the palace as king, displacing the legitimate future heir, the child Alfonso. Later that year however, the impostor was "exposed and executed." [86]

The play was written in 1621 or 1622 according to Bruerton. Juan de Mariana does not name the impostor, but Alarcón calls him Nuño Aulaga, a nobleman who discovers that his family is dishonored since his wife, Teodora, had had a relationship with another man, Bermudo, prior to their marriage. Loyal vassal to Alfonso I, Nuño joined the monarch in the battle against the Moors and was with the King at the time of his death. He buried him after taking his ring and other pieces of identification which he later uses in his scheme to convince the kingdom of Aragón that he was in fact Alfonso I. Ashamed to face the dishonor awaiting him at home, Nuño had spent the intervening years as a pilgrim. Later he learns from Pedro Ruiz de Azagra that the kingdom of Aragón is in a state of turmoil due to the fact that Queen Petronila wishes to cede power to her eleven-year-old son. The nobles are violently opposed to this plan, claiming that she should marry one of them instead and continue to reign. (The situation is very much like that of Tirso's *La prudencia en la mujer.*) The nobles are ambitious and overbearing, each one attempting to gain control of the kingdom through marriage with Queen Petronila. Castro Leal explains that "Los nobles de esta comedia viven, como los de la corte de Felipe III, en una especie de atonía moral."[87] The word *ambición* is repeatedly mentioned in the play, which is a clear indication of Alarcón's intention to satirize the greed and lust for power which characterized the courtiers of his day. There is only one glimmer of hope among all this avarice. He is Sancho Aulaga, son of Nuño, who, although least in rank, is the Queen's sole supporter.

Nuño seizes the opportunity to attempt to convince everyone that he is Alfonso I, thus giving himself the means to avenge his dishonor since under this disguise no one would suspect his true identity. With the appearance of the impostor, all the ministers are quick to swear their allegiance to the fake "Alfonso" and desert the Queen except, of course, for Sancho, whose sense of loyalty to the Queen is a deliberate contrast to the unfaithfulness and self-interest of the other ministers.

Sancho is the only one aware of the true identity of the impostor; he is his father Nuño Aulaga. Sancho, a man of honor, is distressed that his own flesh and blood could possibly scheme such a treacherous act. Nuño, on the other hand, suffers no remorse for his actions since he is a man with one goal in life. A man of Machiavellian principles (or lack of principle, as the anti-Machiavellian critic would maintain), which allege that the end always justifies the means, he only desires to avenge the family dishonor, with no attention to political morality. He is an interesting character whose sense of conjugal honor is so great that he attempts to overthrow the lawful sovereign in his effort to achieve revenge. Perhaps the intention here is to satirize the extremity of Nuño's adherence to the honor code. Is it not a more serious offense in

Alarcón's eyes for Nuño to pretend to be king? Mariana clearly states his advocacy of hereditary succession in order to maintain order in Chapter III of the first book of *De rege*: "Hé aquí por qué casi todas las monarquías han sido al fin hereditarias, y á naciones perpetuas han sido dados príncipes en cierto modo perpetuos, cosa para todos sumamente ventajosa."[88] Bodin, as Reynolds remarks, also believed that "power should descend from father to son in order to avoid the dangers of an interregnum and other weaknesses so apparent in Poland and in the Holy Roman Empire."[89] Alarcón must have agreed with these political beliefs and therefore this character, who dared to overthrow a legitimate monarch, is a tyrant in the old Greek sense of the word and must suffer the consequences and face a tragic end. In the second act, Sancho, as spokesman for Alarcón, says:

> Si ser por reinar [traidor]
> dijo que es lícito alguno,
> fue cuando la [tiranía]
> daba los cetros del mundo;
> fue cuando idólatras pechos
> no temieron ser perjuros;
> fue cuando el vasallo al rey
> natural amor no tuvo;
> mas hoy, que la sucesión
> les da derecho tan justo;
> hoy, que el amor se deriva,
> por legítimo transcurso,
> de los padres a los hijos;
> hoy, que del cristiano yugo
> a cumplir los juramentos
> obligan los estatutos,
> ¿cómo por reinar podrá
> decir que es lícito alguno
> ser [traidor], sino quien tenga,
> lejos del cristiano culto,
> mucha ambición, poca ley,
> sangre vil y pecho bruto? (vss.1601–1622); [emphasis added][90]

Ultimately, Nuño is placed in prison for attempting to kill his wife's past lover, Bermudo. Sancho goes to visit his father in prison and gives him a dagger with which to kill himself in order to avoid an ignominious death on the gallows. His father requests that Sancho kill him and

Sancho obeys. Obedience to the father, according to Bodin, is part of the natural order of things and should therefore be respected.[91]

Later, Sancho learns, however, that he is not the son of Nuño and that his real father is Bermudo, thus making it impossible for him to marry the woman he loves, Teresa, Bermudo's daughter, who is his half-sister. It is a shame that Sancho, of such noble character, cannot be rewarded with her hand in marriage. Most critics consider it an error on Alarcón's part that he altered the parentage of Sancho. Castro Leal suggests that Alarcón perhaps made this alteration in the story in order to show that the noble and upright Sancho could not have descended from the traitor Nuño.[92] Poesse, on the other hand, points out the fact that Bermudo does not offer a favorable image of a father either, since he had enjoyed an extramarital affair with Teodora. He is convinced that Alarcón should have had second thoughts about a son's murdering a father.[93] It is hard to accept a man who commits patricide as a virtuous noble; if the man murdered was not his father, the crime seems perhaps less appalling. It appears most convincing that Sancho may have committed this murder not only in obedience to his "father's" wishes (since at the time of the crime Sancho believed Nuño to be his father), but as the only method by which to protect the Queen and the legitimate heir to the throne. Horrified by his father's treacherous attempt to overthrow a natural monarch, he felt there was no recourse but to kill the traitor. Extreme loyalty and the desire to save the reputation and honor of his sovereign can be explained as the motivating force behind Lycurgus's suicide in *El dueño de las estrellas*. Similarly, Sancho, a truly loyal subject, murders his "father" in an attempt to protect the legitimate monarch. The play is once again built on the cornerstone of Alarcón's political philosophy—the vassal's duty to put the interests of the nation's legitimate ruler above all other principles. As it turns out, however, Sancho is not guilty of patricide, and he has heroically rid the country of a traitor. Even though the dramatist in all probability felt that Nuño's tragic death at the hands of his "son" was well deserved, with his characteristic temperance, Alarcón altered Sancho's paternity in order to remove any hint of blemish from Sancho's outstanding character.

In *El dueño de las estrellas* Lycurgus, in the final act, announces some reformatory statutes for the land of Crete; in this play certain reform measures are also suggested by the *gracioso* Zaratán (vss. 2039–2108). As might be expected, Zaratán's reforms are not as serious as those of Lycurgus, a historic lawgiver. They are mostly of a less sweeping and fundamental nature than Lycurgus's but some of them still echo the proposals of Pérez de Herrera and others. The first of the several laws that he would like to see enacted is that the lawyer of the losing party pay all the costs of the lawsuit: the number of suits would be reduced and lawyers would exert more care in the preparation of their cases. Produce which is still unripe should be sold at a lesser price than mature fruit which can be consumed immediately. Sons of farmers and artisans should not be permitted to study letters or be appointed to the bench because of the scarcity of these laborers. This is a constantly repeated reform measure in Alarcón's plays which is indicative of Pérez de Herrera's profound influence upon this dramatist. Pérez de Herrera suggested that there not be so many teachers and schools of grammar where the common people would go to learn a little Latin, and then, for their convenience, become priests or monks, leaving, in many cases, their land uncultivated. The dramatist's serious concern about the agricultural and commercial decline of Spain is apparent in this law, though the cynical suggestion here is that these people would also be thieves in office. Next, those who gamble or who play cards, he slyly suggests, should not be arrested since card-selling is licensed by the state. Taxes should also not be levied on the necessities of life but on coaches, ornaments on clothing, games, parties, dances and excursions (vss. 2070–2078), in other words, on non-essential luxuries and diversions. The King should also sell positions and offices because "habrá mil que las compren" (vs. 2078). Poesse indicates that Alarcón had not yet received the position which he sought ceaselessly for many years and perhaps included this as one of the laws of Zaratán's kingdom to help appease some of his bitter feelings.[94] As we have seen, he was not successful in achieving a government post until 1626. Mistresses of married men should not be exiled from Court, since the men will only follow them, leaving their wives to fend for themselves. This reform proposal reflects Pérez de Herrera's concern for the poor women of the nation. He suggested that convents be established where poor noblewomen and divorced women could be kept decently and without scandal. Men should also not fill positions that are women's work : ..."que un barbón que ser pudiera / soldado o labrador, no es bien que venda / hilo y seda sentado en una tienda." (vss. 2087–2089).

Minor complaints about some of the incongruities and inconveniences of court life include the following: Owners of roof terraces who rent them during bullfights and other *fiestas* should collect their fees on the ground floor rather than the terrace itself, where the poor customer will pay an exorbitant sum rather than climb down so many stairs; those lucky enough to have Court positions should not claim they are rendering services since they have asked the Crown to grant them these posts as a favor; because gambling houses apparently can never be eliminated, the office of casino owner should be sold by the Crown; finally, prostitutes should be required to wander the streets veiled so that virtuous women will then, to preserve their good name, dispense with veils.

At the end of the play peace is restored as the boy Alfonso is proclaimed king and his mother, Petronila, abdicates. The rule of the legitimate king has been a major concern throughout the play and for Alarcón, this play could not possibly end in any other way. The new sovereign also awards Sancho the honors he deserves.

2. No hay mal que por bien no venga

This is the final play of the Mexican dramatist that will be considered here. It was published in 1653, in the *Laurel de comedias. Quarta parte de diferentes autores*. There is, however, no absolute proof that this play was written by Alarcón. The exact date of composition remains a mystery, but Castro Leal places it somewhere between 1623 and 1625.[95] Poesse cites Bonilla y San Martín, who makes a convincing argument that the play must have been written sometime around the beginning of 1623, since in Act I the *golilla* is mentioned and that was the year this small rigid collar was first worn.[96]

Alarcón again uses Mariana as his source for the history of don García, son of King Alfonso III (866–910) of León, who conspired to overthrow his own father with the aid of various ministers and nobles. Don García was captured and placed in prison in the castle of Gauzón. Nuño Hernández, father-in-law of Prince García, continued the attempt to overthrow the legitimate monarch. With the help of the queen and her two other sons, he made war against Alfonso for two years. Finally, weary of conflict, Alfonso renounced the throne in favor of his son García, whose rule ironically lasted a short three years, since he died in 914.[97] Alarcón's play treats this episode only through the imprisonment of the rebellious prince and does not consider the ensuing history, which would have been anticlimactic.

This, like *La crueldad por el honor,* is an important play since it reveals the dramatist's political beliefs concerning the natural sucession of kings. It is also valuable to examine this work because it deals with some of the same king-*privado* problems which have been the focus of attention in other political plays studied here.

The play takes place in Zamora, and Act I begins on a comical note as it introduces two interesting characters, don Juan and don Domingo de don Blas. Don Juan, though a nobleman, is a trickster and a thief who will do anything to win the hand of Leonor, daughter of don Ramiro, who is the *privado* of Prince García. Later he even attempts to rob Ramiro in order to have money enough to marry Leonor. He rents a house which he does not own to don Domingo de don Blas, the other entertaining character, whose idiosyncrasies make him unique. Act I is also utilized by the dramatist to poke fun at some of the styles and customs of seventeenth-century Spain. Don Domingo is an eccentric man who considers comfort his first priority and pays no attention to fashion. For example, he refuses to stand below his lady's window all night long for fear of catching a chill. He is also seen publicly without the fashionable large-brimmed hat, which he finds to be of extravagant proportions, nor does he wear the customary *golilla.* He tells the hat maker in no uncertain terms:

> El vestido ha de servir
> de ornato y comodidad;
> pues si basta la mitad
> deste sombrero a cumplir
> con el uno y otro intento
> ¿para qué es bueno que ande,
> si me lo pongo tan grande,
> forcejando con el viento;... (vss. 713–720)[98]

He also ridicules the oversized clothing worn by many and considered modish:

> El vestido pienso yo
> que ha de imitar nuestra hechura;
> porque si nos desfigura,
> es disfraz, que ornato no. (vss. 725–728)

He further explains that he refuses to spend money on items which cause him discomfort: "...que no quiero / comprar yo por mi dinero / cosa que me cause enfado" (vss. 730–732).

Don Domingo later goes to have a new cloak made for himself. The tailor advises him that the current style is to wear the cloak ankle length. Domingo is outraged and refuses to yield to the pressures of fashion: "La capa que el más curioso / y el más grave ha de traer, / modesto adorno ha de ser, / y no embarazo penoso" (vss. 789–792), adding that it would be impossible to ride a horse, to kneel, and to fight without feeling hampered by a cloak at such a ridiculous length. He boldly defies the fashion trend and orders the tailor to shorten the cloak: "Así ha de ser: / vos tendréis menos que hacer, / y yo menos que pagar" (vss. 810–812).

Domingo is a man who is always concerned about his convenience and comfort, so it is not surprising that he is also adverse to steps. He searches for a place to live without stairs:

> que en bajo quiero vivir,
> porque, en habiendo escalera,
> no me atrevo a salir fuera
> por no volverla a subir. (vss. 829–832)

This statement recalls the *gracioso* Zaratán's comment in *La crueldad por el honor*, who similarly complains about the number of steps needed to climb in order to view a performance of a play or other event. With similar concern for comfort, he also seeks a residence distanced from gardens and fountains, where mosquitoes, birds and children would irritate him. Likewise he refuses to live anywhere near a carpenter, blacksmith, a belfry or carriage house for fear of the noise level.

The name Domingo, although a common Spanish name, may have been a deliberate choice of the playwright. It seems fitting that such a man with lust for comfort and convenience would be called by the name Domingo, which is also, coincidentally, the day of the week which God, as is stated in Genesis 2:2 and 2:3, blessed and sanctified as the day of rest. Don Domingo is certainly a man who stresses the importance of rest. Alarcón has created this hilarious eccentric in order to entertain his audience, but one must not overlook the underlying intention to satirize the extravagant spending on fashion while the nation suffered from economic decline. The dramatist's concerns are similar to those of the Junta, but he hoped to convey this serious message by way of an amusing character.

Act II begins to take on a more serious tone. The personality of Domingo also begins to change. Leonor loves Juan in spite of his character flaws, and now she considers their union more favorably after she overhears the conversation between Juan and Domingo over the rental of the house which Juan pretends to own. She believes Juan is a wealthy man. Domingo remains a steadfast nonconformist as he enters Scene 3 of Act II "con capa hasta la espada, sombrero muy bajo y de muy poca halda y valona sin golilla" (p. 117). In the following scene the careful reader may begin to notice the development of this character from an eccentric man with strange idiosyncrasies to that of a prudent man who, although he has been a valiant soldier, finds the danger of the bullring to be an unnecessarily risky challenge: "No he de arriesgar con los toros / la vida:..."(vss. 1333–1334). This prudent manner of thinking reminds us of Don Quijote's explanation of true valor. He says that valor "...es una virtud que está puesta entre dos extremos viciosos, como son la cobardía y la temeridad;"[99] Alarcón slowly reveals the true character of Domingo. As the play progresses, he begins to appear more prudent than perverse.

Domingo later refuses to eat at the customary hour, insisting that his stomach is not controlled by the clock. He will eat when he is hungry and not at some designated hour. He comes to the lucid conclusion that people should not feel tied to social customs and to have to do exactly as everyone else does:

> El manjar me sabe más
> cuando yo le he menester,
> y no tengo de comer
> porque comen los demás.
> El uso común dispuso
> hora en esto señalada,
> voluntaria, no forzada.
> No ha de obligarnos el uso;... (vss. 1660–1667)

People should not behave unnaturally because of social pressure and a foolish respect for conformity.

In Act II Alarcón repeats the satire of a society where success is measured on the basis of what one possesses rather than on personal accomplishment and virtue. It is a criticism which appears in all of his works:

> Para serlo [mejor que otro] basta ser
> el más rico; bien lo fundo,
> puesto que no tiene el mundo
> más linaje que "tener". (vss.1365–1368);[emphasis added]

Act III is the most serious of the three acts, and the true depth of character of both Domingo and Juan is discovered here. The reader or spectator is now able to perceive the underlying prudence and rationality behind Domingo's apparent eccentricity. In this act, Juan, the ultimate trickster, will be transformed by the wisdom and example of Domingo. Prince García, aided by other influential citizens of Zamora, including the greedy and ambitious Ramiro, prepares the revolt against his father. Complications arise when Domingo refuses to assist with the conspiracy. He is locked up in Ramiro's house so that their evil plans cannot be thwarted. It is providential that Juan comes at this moment to rob Ramiro's house, for he finds Domingo imprisoned there. Domingo tells Juan of the traitorous intentions of García, who is attempting to overthrow the *rey natural*. He explains that although García is heir to the throne, his time has not yet come to inherit the Crown. The dramatist's political conviction about the natural hereditary succession of kings is again repeated. In *La crueldad por el honor*, as we have seen, Sancho is honored for having rid the country of a tyrant who attempts to overthrow the legitimate monarch. Similarly, Domingo awakens "el leal heroico pecho" of Juan, pleading with him to help him put a stop to this violation of "la ley humana y la divina." It is their obligation as vassals to do something about the situation. Ramiro, he says, is breaking the faith which he owes to the King by taking part in this conspiracy to overthrow Alfonso III. As *privado* to García, it is his job to direct the Prince on the right path rather than, for the sake of power and wealth, to give in to the Prince's wayward designs. Once again we meet an evil *privado* who, for reasons of ambition, leads a prince astray. Afraid to jeopardize his position at Court, Ramiro not only permits the Prince to have his way but helps him in his attempt to accomplish the treacherous act. The *privado* should be a source of wise counsel to the Prince rather than an accessory to his crime. He must be someone who is untainted with self-interest. In Act I, Ramiro's selfish intentions are clearly stated:

> Del Rey don Alonso estoy
> mal satisfecho; y García,
> pues que de mí tanto fía
> y tan su privado soy,
>   pondrá en mi mano el gobierno
> del reino, y, con su poder
> y mi industria, podré hacer
> mi casa y mi nombre eterno. (vss. 337–344)

Juan is impressed by the wisdom of Domingo and is instantly converted to the cause of legitimacy:

> ¡Ah, ilustre caballero!
> ¡Oh, en el valor y la lealtad primero!
> ¿Qué espíritu divino,
> qué aliento celestial, a vuestros labios
> consejos dicta en mi favor tan sabios,
> que, no sólo a mi ciego desatino
> dan arrepentimiento,
> pero sin el castigo el escarmiento? (vss. 2230–2237)

Juan feels redeemed by the purifying spirit of Domingo, which is rooted in loyalty to King Alfonso: "Por vos gané lo que por mí he perdido: / seré muriendo el que naciendo he sido" (vss. 2238–2239). He repeats the remarkable transformation of his spirit in the following scene: "Ya los cielos / mi inclinación mudaron, / que al fuego de lealtad me acrisolaron" (vss. 2274–2276), which his servant Beltrán finds amazing: "Si tú vas convertido, yo admirado / de ver tan valeroso acomodado" (vss. 2280–2281).

The reformed Juan goes to inform Alfonso of the conspiracy planned against him by his own son. Juan proves to be a loyal subject even in the face of danger of retaliation on the part of García. Awakened by the counsel of Domingo, he proves his loyalty even at the risk of losing Leonor forever. Ramiro would never consent to his marriage with Leonor now that he has spoiled their treacherous plan. The King praises his valor, which is responsible for saving his legitimate position: "Vuestro valor / el remedio me asegura" (vss. 2604–2605).

The end of this play is similar to the others of this study as the King dispenses justice to all of the characters. Prince García is imprisoned for his plot to overthrow the King, but Ramiro is forgiven for his part in the conspiracy so as not to dishonor his daughter Leonor, who will marry the reformed Juan. Juan, a man lacking in material wealth, has proven himself to be an honorable man deserving of her hand. He is, however, awarded two towns of his choice within the kingdom, thus making him a rich man, and he is also rewarded with the position of *privado* and friend of the King. Juan is the ideal choice for *privado* in the eyes of Alarcón. Since he has not been motivated by ambition or greed in his service to the King, the kingdom will profit from the wise counsel he will give the monarch. Don Domingo is responsible for having transformed the once criminal Juan into an honorable man well suited for the position of *privado* to the King and is himself given the hand of Constanza, cousin of Leonor, whom he loves.

The play therefore comes to an appropriate conclusion. Alarcón's purpose was to illustrate the damaging influence of an ambitious minister upon royalty by contrasting him with a man whose innate sense of responsibility to the Crown far surpasses any desire for personal gain. The inherent valor and virtue of a seemingly eccentric man and his influence upon Juan is responsible for saving the King's legitimate position. One should not evaluate the virtue of a person solely by appearance alone. One's character cannot be measured by his conformity to social pressures. Instead, Alarcón illustrates that goodness and valor stem from being able to discern right from wrong and acting accordingly, with no regard to social pressure.

NOTES

[1] For a general consideration of the life and work of Alarcón, see Willard F. King, *Juan Ruiz de Alarcón, letrado y dramaturgo* (Mexico: Colegio de México, 1989), especially Ch. IV (for the training and mentality of the lawyer), Ch. VII (for the duties of a *relator*), and Appendix A (for the known dates of performance of Alarcón's plays).

[2] Mary Austin Cauvin, O.P. "The Comedia de Privanza in the Seventeenth Century," Diss. U of Pennsylvania 1957, pp. 203, 276, 280, 283, 394, 402, 414 (Montalbán) and pp. 121, 145, 154, 175, 218, 330, 367, 388, 442, 451 (Lope).

[3] Willard King, "Alarcón's *Ganar Amigos*: The King, the Privado, and the Law," pp. 77–88 in *Texto y Espectáculo*, ed. Barbara Mujica (New York: UP of America, 1989), p.77.

[4] A. Robert Lauer, "The Use and Abuse of History in the Spanish Theater of the Golden Age: The Regicide of Sancho II as treated by Juan de la Cueva, Guillén de Castro, and Lope de Vega," *Hispanic Review*, 56 (1988), pp. 17–37.

[5] Lindenberger, p. 5.

[6] Lauer, p. 19.

[7] Lauer, p. 33.

[8] Lindenberger, p. 8.

[9] Lindenberger, p. 115.

[10] Lindenberger, p. 8.

[11] Niceto Alcalá-Zamora y Torres, *El derecho y sus colindancias en el teatro de don Juan Ruiz de Alarcón* (Mexico: Imprenta Universitaria, 1949), pp. 11–18.

[12] Alcalá-Zamora, p. 26.

[13] Alcalá-Zamora, p. 27.

[14] Alcalá-Zamora, p. 38.

[15] Agustín Millares Carlo, "Prólogo" in *Obras Completas de Juan Ruiz de Alarcón*, vol. 1, ed. Agustín Millares Carlo (México: Fondo de Cultura Económica, 1957), p. xxix (Millares Carlo is citing Professor Courtney Bruerton; Bruerton's dating is accepted for all of the Alarcón plays studied here.)

[16] King, *Juan Ruiz de Alarcón*, Appendix A.

[17] King, "La ascendencia paterna de Juan Ruiz de Alarcón y Mendoza," *Nueva Revista de Filología Hispánica*, 19 (1970), p. 81.

[18] Juan Ruiz de Alarcón, *Los favores del mundo* in *Obras Completas*, vol. 1, ed. Agustín Millares Carlo (Mexico: Fondo de Cultura Económica, 1957), p. 29. (All further citations of this play refer to this edition.)

[19] Díez Borque, p. 100.

[20] Alcalá-Zamora, p. 43.

[21] Díez Borque, p. 142.

[22] Maravall, p. 78.

[23] The typical Alarconian heroine is virtuous and resolute. She is outspoken about her convictions and willingly expresses her viewpoints without persuasion. She is an admirable character and can be seen in several of the political plays studied here. She first appears here in *Los favores del mundo* in the character of Anarda who refuses to wed to a man she does not love, or to be placed in a convent without a true vocation (see pp. 81–82). We meet her again *La amistad castigada* as Aurora, where she expresses dissatisfaction for the reprehensible behavior of Dionysius (see pp. 96–97). Like a lawyer, she offers legal documentation maintaining that the law should decide the punishment (see pp. 100–101). Again we can find her in *Los pechos privilegiados* in the character of Elvira who, like Aurora, disapproves of the monarch's perverse behavior. She chides King Alfonso for his ill-conduct insisting that she will not enter into any relationship with him out of wedlock (see pp. 114 and 120). As spokesman for Alarcón, the noble heroine is always a source of inspiration for the other characters in the play.

24 Plutarch, *Lives*, trans. John Langhorne and William Langhorne (Philadelphia: Brannan and Morford, 1811), vol. 1, p. 100.

25 John Langhorne and William Langhorne, Introduction to Plutarch's *Lives*, vol. 1, pp. lxxvii–lxxviii.

26 Plutarch, vol. 1, pp. 102–104.

27 Alarcón, *El dueño de las estrellas* in *Obras Completas*, vol. 2, ed. Agustín Millares Carlo (Mexico: Fondo de Cultura Económica, 1959), pp. 43–47. (All further citations of this play refer to this edition.)

28 Plutarch, vol. 1, pp. 103–107.

29 Plutarch, vol. 1, p. 107.

30 Plutarch, vol. 1, pp. 119; see also vol. 8, p. 220.

31 Plutarch, vol. 1, p. 119.

32 Plutarch, vol. 1, p. 119.

33 Plutarch, vol. 1, pp. 108–109.

34 Plutarch, vol. 1, pp. 120–128.

35 Plutarch, vol. 1, p. 136.

36 Plutarch, vol. 1, p. 137.

37 Plutarch, vol. 1, pp. 137–138.

38 Plutarch, vol. 1, p. 140.

39 Plutarch, vol. 1, p. 143.

40 Plutarch, vol. 1, p. 143.

41 Plutarch, vol. 1, p. 144.

42 Plutarch, vol. 1, p. 146.

43 Elliott, *The Count-Duke*, p. 24.

44 Elliott, *The Count-Duke*, p. 84.

45 Jonathan Brown and John H. Elliott, *A Palace for a King* (New Haven, London: Yale UP, 1980), p. 24.

46 Elliott, *The Count-Duke*, p. 104.

47 González Palencia, p. 443.

48 Michel Cavillac, "Introducción" to Cristóbal Pérez de Herrera's *Amparo de pobres* (Madrid: Espasa-Calpe, S.A., 1975), pp. cxci–cxcii.

49 Alcalá-Zamora, p. 56.

50 Alcalá-Zamora, p. 57.

51 Elliott, *The Count-Duke*, pp. 34–45.

52 Elliott, *The Count-Duke*, p. 45.

53 Alcalá-Zamora, p. 25.

54 Bodin, pp. 221–222.

55 Walter Poesse, *Juan Ruiz de Alarcón* (New York: Twayne Publishers, Inc., 1972), p. 62.

56 Plutarch, vol. 7, pp. 148–152.

57 Plutarch, vol. 7, p. 157.

58 Plutarch, vol. 7, pp. 158–165.

59 Alarcón, *La amistad castigada* in *Obras Completas*, vol. 2, ed. Agustín Millares Carlo (Mexico: Fondo de Cultura Económica, 1959), p. 102. (All further citations of this play refer to this edition.) In the play the tyrant's name is, of course, Dionisio; I continue, for the sake of simplicity, to use the classical form of the name.

60 Plutarch, vol. 7, p. 175.

61 Díez Borque, p. 152.

62 Díez Borque, p. 160.

63 A. Robert Lauer, *Tyrannicide and Drama* (Stuttgart: Franz Steiner Verlag Wiesbaden Gmbh, 1987), p. 120.

64 Alcalá-Zamora, p. 45 and p. 49.

65 Alcalá-Zamora, p. 50.

66 King, *"Ganar Amigos,"* p. 78.

67 Alarcón, *"Ganar amigos"* in *Obras Completas*, vol. 2, ed. Agustín Millares Carlo (Mexico: Fondo de Cultura Económica, 1959), p. 295. (All further citations of this play refer to this edition.)

68 King, *"Ganar amigos,"* pp. 78–79.

69 King, *"Ganar amigos,"* p. 79.

70 King, *"Ganar amigos,"* p. 80.

71 José Antonio Maravall, *La Teoría del estado en el siglo XVII* (Madrid: Instituto de Estudios Políticos, 1944), pp. 330–331.

72 Alcalá-Zamora, p. 51.

73 King, *"Ganar amigos,"* p. 81.

74 Alcalá-Zamora, p. 26.

75 Alcalá-Zamora, p. 49.

76 King, *"Ganar amigos,"* p. 82.

77 King, *"Ganar amigos,"* p. 84.

78 King, *Juan Ruiz de Alarcón*, p. 19.

79 Millares Carlo, "Noticia" to *Los pechos privilegiados* in *Obras completas*, vol. 2, ed. Agustín Millares Carlo, p. 656.

80 Juan de Mariana, "Historia general de España," in *Biblioteca de Autores Españoles* XXX, (Madrid: M. Rivadeneyra, 1854), p. 237.

81 Millares Carlo, "Noticia" to *Los pechos privilegiados*, p. 656.

[82] Alarcón, *Los pechos privilegiados* in *Obras Completas*, vol. 2, ed. Agustín Millares Carlo (Mexico: Fondo de Cultura Económica, 1959), pp. 679 and 698. (All further citations of this play refer to this edition.)

[83] Lauer, *Tyrannicide and Drama*, p. 120.

[84] Enrique Tierno Galván, "Introducción" to *Antología de escritores políticos del Siglo de Oro*, textos recogidos por Pedro de Vega (Madrid: Clásicos de la Política, 1965), p. 8.

[85] Poesse, p. 84.

[86] Poesse, pp. 84–85.

[87] Antonio Castro Leal, *Juan Ruiz de Alarcón—su vida y su obra* (Mexico: Ediciones Cuadernos Americanos, 1943), p. 172.

[88] Mariana, "Del rey y de la institución real," p. 473.

[89] Reynolds, Introduction to *Method*, p. xix.

[90] Alarcón, *La crueldad por el honor* in *Obras Completas*, vol. 2, ed. Agustín Millares Carlo (Mexico: Fondo de Cultura Económica, 1959), p. 877. (All further citations of this play refer to this edition.)

[91] Jean Bodin, *The Six Bookes*, pp. 368–369.

[92] Castro Leal, p. 173.

[93] Poesse, p. 87.

[94] Poesse, p. 88.

[95] Castro Leal, p. 186.

[96] Poesse, p. 98.

[97] Poesse, p. 96 (citing Mariana, Libro VII, cap. XIX).

[98] Alarcón, *No hay mal que por bien no venga* in *Obras Completas*, vol. 3, ed. Agustín Millares Carlo (Mexico: Fondo de Cultura Económica, 1968), p. 107. (All further citations of this play refer to this edition.)

[99] Miguel de Cervantes Saavedra, *Don Quijote de la Mancha*, ed. Martín de Riquer, Segunda parte (Barcelona: Editorial Juventud, S.A.,1971), pp. 660–661.

CHAPTER VI
CONCLUSION

Alarcón's political dramas display a concern for sound government and reform measures which is far more persistent, consistent, and insistent than that of any of his contemporaries, such as Tirso or Lope. It is clear that he had read widely in the major political treatises of his day. His concern for justice and the general well-being of the Spanish nation motivated him to attempt to awaken the king and the *privado* to the country's desperate situation and the need for reform.

The Mexican dramatist satirically describes— or seriously prescribes solutions for— many problems faced by seventeenth-century Spain. In *Los favores del mundo* and *La crueldad por el honor*, it is the *gracioso*, usually expected to provide only comic relief in seventeenth-century plays, who is chosen by the dramatist to convey serious concerns by not only criticizing various habits of society which are the causes of the decline, but also by offering several suggestions for economic and political reform that are obviously those of Alarcón. In *El dueño de las estrellas,* the Spartan lawgiver Lycurgus, who is said to have been responsible for having made Sparta at one time the dominant state of Greece because of strict discipline and excellent training of soldiers, is chosen to put forward the most serious proposals of reform to be found in any of these dramas (see Ch.V, pp. 88–89). Zaratán, the *gracioso* of *La crueldad por el honor*, also offers reform measures which, although not as serious as those of Lycurgus, still echo the proposals of Pérez de Herrera (see Ch.V, pp. 124–126). In the final play studied, *No hay mal que por bien no venga*, we notice that Alarcón uses one of the most hilarious characters ever created in the Spanish theater, don Domingo de don Blas, in order to convey a serious message to his audience. This character insists upon nonconformity in order to ridicule the trendy fashions, superfluous spending and other pernicious customs of seventeenth-century Spaniards. Conformity to social pressure should not replace reason in their lives (see Ch.V, pp. 127–130). If, however, Alarcón had been first of all a political theorist, he could have written, like so many lawyers before and after him, a treatise on the causes of the decay of the empire, such as Sancho de Moncada's *Restauración política de España*, or on beggary and poverty, such as Pérez de Herrera's *Amparo de pobres*. But he was first of all a dramatist who saw in the history of the past fascinating dramatic conflicts which could interest—and instruct— the avid theater public of his day.

Alarcón was an advocate of divine-right monarchy (or at least saw no alternative to it), and the fact that all of his political dramas are set in the past was prompted, no doubt, by this conviction. This historical setting allowed him to play with somewhat dangerous topics if he wished to do so, without offering direct criticism of the absolute power of the monarch. No Spanish dramatist could expect to have a play produced which criticized, however innocently, the reigning sovereign or indeed, any Catholic monarch of the sixteenth and seventeenth centuries. The historical ambiance also lends a sense of dignity and importance to the action of the play. Alarcón clearly had read classical and national history—Plutarch, Tacitus, Suetonius, Rivadeneyra, and Guicciardini among others—with attention and interest. Julian Franklin explains the significance of this familiarity with history:

> In the later Renaissance it was very seriously assumed that the reading of historians was the ideal form of political and moral education. And with this conviction the study of the past as such took on a status and importance which it had not known in classical antiquity. A complete familiarity with universal history was now regarded as a fundamental obligation of the educated man.[1]

As he read history, he found situations and characters that could be manipulated to demonstrate to the more astute members of his audience his own personal convictions and his own view of the reforms necessary in Spanish economics and politics. Certainly his plays alone are sufficient to counter Leicester Bradner's charge that Spanish plays seldom address "the issues of good and bad government as the English usually do."[2] There is nothing revolutionary or radical in his thought (divine right absolutist monarchy is upheld without question), but what is notable is the constancy with which he returned to his favorite themes and the artful dramatic technique which makes these political plays exciting theater.

Alarcón's dramas *La crueldad por el honor* and *No hay mal que por bien no venga* illustrate the fervent support of the belief in the hereditary succession of kings. Nuño Aulaga, the impostor in the first play, meets with death at the hands of Sancho. His murder can be considered as an ultimate act of loyalty to Queen Petronila on the part of Sancho, who saw death as a fitting punishment for one who dared to attempt to interrupt natural hereditary succession. Prince García is imprisoned in the latter play for his conspiracy to take the throne through a rebellion against his father.

Since he was a supporter of divine-right monarchy, it seems contradictory that Alarcón dared to place evil kings on the stage. In *El dueño de las estrellas, La amistad castigada,* and *Los pechos privilegiados* the king is portrayed in a less than favorable light, unable to control his passion for a young woman. No matter how misguided the intentions of the king, however, Bodinian theory is strongly supported throughout the dramas. The subjects who prove their loyalty and obedience to royal command are always rewarded and never punished even when the intentions of the monarch are far from honorable. In *El dueño de las estrellas,* for example, Palante is pardoned for his involvement with the king in his conspiracy to seduce Diana. Filipo, *privado* to the king in *La amistad castigada,* is exiled from Court for having proven himself disloyal to Dionysius by disclosing secrets of the king's plan to seduce Aurora, while the servant Turpín is praised for his loyalty even when he has aided the lustful king's desires. And the courtier Ricardo is awarded Aurora's hand in marriage at the close of this play since he has proven, beyond a doubt, that he is the most loyal of all the king's men (see Ch.V, p. 101). Similarly in *Los pechos privilegiados* the self-seeking *privado* Ramiro is not punished for having aided the lustful King Alfonso V in his attempt to seduce Elvira, and the servant Nuño is praised even after admitting his reluctant involvement in the conspiracy of the king to seduce this woman (see Ch.V, pp. 114–115 and 120). Obedience to the sovereign, in this play, is stressed by the dramatist even in the most compromising of situations. In *La crueldad por el honor* Sancho Aulaga is highlighted as an exemplary courtier because of his unshakable loyalty to Queen Petronila even when all the others forsake her in their rash decision to shift their allegiance to an impostor pretending to be King Alfonso I (see Ch.V, p. 122).

A man-servant finds himself caught in a comparable situation involving his master. Once again loyalty and obedience are always applauded. Teón's servant in *El dueño de las estrellas* is praised in this play for his loyalty to his master even when Lycurgus's honor is placed in jeopardy (see Ch.V, p. 90).

We should not, however, forget that no attempt is made to spare monarchs criticism for ethical mistakes. Their reprehensible behavior cannot be forgotten. What we are asked to notice especially, however, is the necessity of good advice from ministers and a respect for the law by all in order to curb the excesses of absolute monarchs. As one check on the misguided intentions of a legitimate sovereign, Alarcón accentuates the positive and necesary role of ministers. He created dramas that stress the necessity of wise counsel stemming from a noble *privado*. According to Alarcón, a good *privado* must have certain attributes. First of all, he must be a friend of the king's (the theorists had stressed the necessity of this relationship—see Ch.II, p. 18). For example, in *El dueño de las estrellas,* the king welcomes Lycurgus to the Court as his *privado*, referring to him as *amigo* and *igual* (vss. 938–939). He must also be a disinterested minister whose first priority is a healthy body politic. He must not flatter the king but give prudent advice, even if it is unpleasant at times. King Pedro I in *Ganar amigos* stands out as a virtuous monarch who is guided by the wise counsel of his *privado. Los favores del mundo* gives the example of two ideal *privado*(s), Garci-Ruiz and don Juan, who together offer wise counsel to a prince who learns, with their help, valuable lessons for his future government. In *El dueño de las estrellas* the Spartan lawgiver Lycurgus is the *privado* responsible for giving the sovereign practical advice that will help to revive a declining state. Even in *La crueldad por el honor* and *No hay mal que por bien no venga* the reader and spectator can easily see for themselves that the kingdom which has a loyal and disinterested *privado* at the helm will prosper because of his trusted counsel.

Integrity is another important characteristic of a good *privado* which is stressed in *Los pechos privilegiados* and *No hay mal que por bien no venga*. In both cases such integrity is viewed not only as the ultimate indication of a man's ability to serve as *privado* to the king, but also as a means by which to measure success. Integrity is demonstrated when the minister refuses to carry out orders or fabricate schemes which would undermine his own conscience. The noble *privado*, following Bodinian theory, realizes that the subject does not have to obey an unjust command. He simply cannot lay violent hands on his monarch or rebel against him. In *Los pechos privilegiados,* Rodrigo, the exemplary courtier, disobeys royal command by refusing to help Alfonso V with his plans to seduce Elvira. Also Count Melendo does not allow the king to corrupt his daughter. He decides to relinquish his citizenship in order to protect his family honor from the lustful king (see Ch.V, p. 117).

An especially model *privado* is depicted in *Ganar amigos*, in which blind and injudicious obedience to the king is not advocated when the welfare of the nation as a whole is at stake. Fadrique, a wise *privado*, realizes that he must put aside the command of the king for the greater good of the entire country (see Ch.V, p. 106). Only the most exemplary of courtiers are allowed to make the decision to disregard the commands of the sovereign for the greater good of the nation. These men utilize their innate gift of reason in deciding what is best for the country.

La amistad castigada introduces both a good and a bad *privado*: Dionysius, an evil king, dismisses the good *privado* and chooses instead the spineless Filipo. The King himself is deposed and exiled at the end, and the virtuous *privado* Dión becomes the new king. *Los pechos privilegiados* also illustrates the damaging effects of a *privado puro* who caters to the whims of a lustful sovereign for the sake of personal advancement. When the kingdom lacks the guidance of a wise counselor, or if the *privado* is disloyal, scheming, and untrustworthy, the king and the state are at peril.

The appeal to the law, both natural and written, in order to maintain the health of the state, is yet another check on the monarch, and is a dominant theme in Alarcón's political plays. In *Ganar amigos* the *gracioso* Encinas declares that when a decree is publicly announced, the king has then placed his own authority behind it and therefore cannot break his given word. Thus the king is bound by his own laws (see Ch.V, p. 110). More than other playwrights of the time, Alarcón also strongly advocates the equality of all citizens under the law. Everyone, including the king and all his subjects, nobles and the common people alike, must be treated equally under the law.[3] In this respect the dramatist favors the theory of Mariana, which states that the king is not responsible only to God (as Bodin believes him to be), but is equally responsible, as are his subjects, to the laws of the land. Therefore, in *La amistad castigada* the power of the law is responsible for the fulfillment of justice, and both the minister Filipo and King Dionysius are exiled for their crimes, providing the solution for the play's conflicts. Servants are also treated as equals in these political dramas. In *Ganar amigos* the *gracioso*

Encinas claims that servants are as honorable and virtuous as are the nobles. All servants, he says, are equal to their masters, not in material wealth but certainly with regard to their honor (Act III, Sc. 8). Alcalá-Zamora remarks that the dramatist's sympathy for those of humble birth is manifest in the fact that the servants in Alarcón's dramas are generally the spokesmen of sincerity.[4] They often speak reasonably about important issues. This uniqueness of Alarcón's servants is also commented upon by Poesse: "To Alarcón, poverty was especially bitter because it obscured in the eyes of others, he thought, what was noble in a person, whether of ancestry or of character."[5]

It is not only servants but also women— who in seventeenth-century Spain had so little liberty or protection before the law—who are given special protection and consideration in these political dramas. Again and again it is emphasized that women should be given freedom of choice in matters of marriage and love. *Los favores del mundo, El dueño de las estrellas, La amistad castigada, Ganar amigos,* and *Los pechos privilegiados* all include strong-minded women who take charge of their lives by either resisting pressure from a concupiscent king who desires to seduce them, or by insisting that they have the right to select their own husbands. The power of natural law as a check upon the king is clear in *El dueño de las estrellas.* Diana resists the advances of the lustful king following her instincts of *natural razón,* which does not permit love and lust to coexist in one man's heart. Even the king is subject to the rule of natural law, which forbids forcible rape of a woman. Repeatedly the reader is reminded that the king, although he is divinely appointed, is, nevertheless, bound by natural law, and his subjects do not have to accept the unjust behavior of the sovereign towards them. Alarcón has aptly utilized the figure of the offended woman to act as his spokesman for the responsibility of the king to natural law.

Clemency and forgiveness on the part of the powerful likewise is a dominant theme in these dramas. In *Los favores del mundo* and *Ganar amigos* the *privado*(s) Garci-Ruiz and Fadrique are portrayed as models of forgiveness. They both find themselves to be more satisfied with the act of pardon than with cold revenge. It is no accident that these men are also exemplary individuals who display a keen sense of integrity, and who are able to utilize their God-given gift of reason to its fullest advantage. Garci-Ruiz is awarded the post of *privado* by Prince Henry, who discovers that Garci-Ruiz is capable of forgiving don Juan even though, some time earlier, he had committed an affront against Garci-Ruiz. The Prince finds the new impulse toward tempered justice to be refreshing. Fadrique in *Ganar amigos* likewise shocks the Court with his clemency when he openly forgives Fernando for having killed his brother in a fight over doña Flor. He teaches the Court of Pedro I that it is not always wise to impose the sternest possible law. The law must at times yield to an even higher principle of reason of state (vss. 1949–1950).[6] Fadrique, in the end, benefits from his own prudent counsel. Both Garci-Ruiz and Fadrique are portrayed as prudent ministers who are able to discern when clemency, if the law allows it, is more suitable than Draconian punishment. The justice of Lycurgus in *El dueño de las estrellas* is also tempered with mercy toward the servant who has not actually planned the offense against Lycurgus but has only assisted his master out of loyalty.

Another restraint on the king's power is the force of public opinion. In *Los pechos privilegiados* the fallen *privado* is reinstated in power by the king, because the people desire it. The king recognizes, reluctantly, that a sovereign's rule may be dangerously questioned by the people if he blatantly ignores their disapproval of his selfish and unjust actions. This is the only play in which this check is mentioned (see Ch.V, p. 119).

Active rebellion and deposition of a ruler do actually occur in *La amistad castigada*. The dramatist has chosen for this drama the historically infamous Dionysius, "Tyrant of Syracuse," who held the throne illegitimately. Dionysius is exiled by a group of nobles because he has proven himself to be a tyrant in both senses, i.e., as a ruler who possesses the throne illegitimately and as one who abuses the rights of his subjects. And characteristically, Alarcón finds the power to depose the king in the *law* (in this case a law against ingratitude). The dramatization of a successful and justified rebellion against a reigning monarch makes this play unusually interesting. *La amistad castigada* can be viewed as a cautionary play for unprincipled monarchs, since Bodin warned that royal crimes could incite such rebellion, and Mariana, as we know, claimed such resistance as the peoples' right.

In sum, the plays studied here reveal serious and persistent consideration of the problem of an absolutist, hereditary, divine-right monarchy, understood in Bodinian terms. The system is never questioned; on the contrary, the inviolability of the legitimate monarch's person and privileges is sustained time and time again.

Still, the major problem considered is modes of dealing with individual monarchs who are oblivious to the needs and rights of their subjects. The first necessity is an upright and courageous *privado* willing to counsel the king bravely. If the *privado* is evil and the king is evil, disaster will ensue (see *La amistad castigada*). If the *privado* is honorable and courageous, the king will utimately mend his ways and a healthy state will be restored.

Beyond the central role of the *privado*, a further check on the sovereign is the power of the law itself, beginning with natural law, which, as Bodin asserted, cannot be ignored by a ruler (see *El dueño de las estrellas* and *La amistad castigada*). There is likewise the force of public opinion, a major factor in curbing royal abuses (see *Los pechos privilegiados*). And finally, perhaps most importantly, there is the legal code of the state, to which, Alarcón insists (tempering Bodinian doctrine with Mariana's theories), the king himself is subject (in two plays, *Ganar amigos* and *La amistad castigada,* specific laws of the kingdom affect the harmonious final resolution of the play's conflicts). Before the law, all citizens are, or should be, equal, and in its provisions a citizen may hope to find not severe punishment but true and clement justice. It is in the insistence on the power and utility of the law in an absolutist state that Alarcón —Licentiate in Law from the University of Mexico—makes his most outstanding contribution to the political drama of his day.

Primarily, these plays, so serious in subject matter, are and were meant to be exciting dramas whose conflicts the young bureaucrats and officials in the theater audience would necessarily find interesting. Further, of course, since the Madrid courtiers who attended plays gossiped constantly about the king, his ministers, and possible changes in government, such political plays were bound to hold their interest. Because they deal with court life, they might also be especially attractive to those selecting dramas to be played at Court (and several of these plays were). Beyond that, Alarcón may, in some real sense, have hoped to remind Philip IV and Olivares of the perils of *privanza* and irresponsible sovereigns. In order to suit the dramatist's design, he portrayed the contrasting methods of very different kinds of ministers. Alarcón offered alternatives from which Olivares himself must choose. As *privado* to Philip IV, he could choose to be a *privado puro*, who, as the *gracioso* of *Los pechos privilegiados* explains, by indulging the king's every desire, produces frequent miscarriages of justice; or he could choose to be a *privado aguado* and greatly assist in the creation of a healthy body politic. The choice was left for Olivares himself to make.

NOTES

[1] Julian H. Franklin, *Jean Bodin and the Sixteenth-Century Revolution in the Methodology of Law and History* (New York and London: Columbia UP, 1963), p. 3.

[2] Bradner, p. 106.

[3] Alcalá-Zamora, pp. 45 and 49.

[4] Alcalá-Zamora, p. 49.

[5] Poesse, p. 34.

[6] King, *"Ganar amigos,"* p. 6.

BIBLIOGRAPHY

Alcalá-Zamora y Torres, Niceto. *El derecho y sus colindancias en el teatro de don Juan Ruiz de Alarcón.* Mexico: Imprenta Universitaria, 1949.

Allen, J. W. *A History of Political Thought in the Sixteenth Century.* London: Methuen & Co., Ltd., 1928.

Blanca de los Ríos, ed., Preámbulo. *La prudencia en la mujer* in *Obras dramáticas completas.* By Tirso de Molina. Madrid: Aguilar, 1958. Vol. 3.

Blecua, José Manuel. Introducción. *Obras Completas.* Vol. 1: *Poesía original.* By Francisco de Quevedo. Barcelona: Editorial Planeta, S.A., 1963. xxxi-xxxvi.

Bodin, Jean. *Method for the Easy Comprehension of History.* Trans. by Beatrice Reynolds. New York: Octagon Books, Inc., 1966.

___.*The Six Bookes of a Commonweale.* 1606; rpt., Ed. Kenneth Douglas McRae. Cambridge: Harvard UP, 1962.

Bradner, Leicester. "The Theme of *Privanza* in Spanish and English Drama 1590–1625." In *Homenaje a William Fichter.* Ed. A. David Kossoff and José Amor y Vázquez. Madrid: Editorial Castalia, 1971. 7–106.

Brown, Jonathan and J.H. Elliott. *A Palace for a King.* New Haven and London: Yale UP, 1980.

Castro Leal, Antonio. *Juan Ruiz de Alarcón—Su vida y su obra.* Mexico: Ediciones Cuadernos Americanos, 1943.

Cauvin, Sister Mary Austin. "The Comedia de Privanza in the Seventeenth Century." Diss. U of Pennsylvania, 1957.

Cavillac, Michel. *Gueux et Marchands dans le "Guzmán de Alfarache."* Bordeaux: Institut d'Études Ibériques et Ibéro-Americaines de L'Université de Bordeaux, 1983.

Cervantes, Miguel de. *Segunda parte del ingenioso hidalgo Don Quijote de la Mancha.* Ed. Martín de Riquer. Barcelona: Editorial Juventud, 1971.

Díez Borque, José María. *Sociología de la comedia española del siglo XVII.* Madrid: Ediciones Cátedra, S.A., 1976.

Elliott, J. H. *The Count-Duke of Olivares. The Statesman in an Age of Decline.* New Haven and London: Yale UP, 1986.

___."Quevedo and the Count-Duke of Olivares." in *Quevedo in Perspective*. Ed. James Iffland. Newark, Del.: Juan de la Cuesta, 1982. 227–250.

___.Richelieu and Olivares. Cambridge: Cambridge UP, 1984.

Espejo, Cristóbal. "Enumeración y atribuciones de algunas juntas de la administración española desde el siglo XVI hasta el año 1800." *Revista de la Biblioteca, Archivo y Museo*, Vol. 8, 32 (1931), 325–362.

Exum, Frances. *The Metamorphosis of Lope de Vega's King Pedro*. Madrid: Colección Plaza Mayor Scholar, 1974.

Figgis, John Neville. *The Divine Right of Kings*. Cambridge: Cambridge UP, 1914.

Fox, Dian. *Kings in Calderón: A Study in Characterization and Political Theory*. London: Tamesis Books Ltd., 1986.

Franklin, Julian H. *Jean Bodin and the Sixteenth-Century Revolution in the Methodology of Law and History*. New York: Columbia UP, 1963.

González Palencia, Angel. *La Junta de Reformación*. Valladolid: La Academia de Estudios Históricos-Sociales de Valladolid, 1932.

Greenleaf, William H., "Bodin and the Idea of Order," In *Jean Bodin*. Munich: Verlag C.H. Beck, 1973. 23–38.

Hamilton, Bernice. *Political Thought in Sixteenth Century Spain*. Oxford: Clarendon Press, 1963.

Hume, Martin. *The Court of Philip IV: Spain in Decadence*. New Ed. New York: Brentano's Publishers, 1927.

___.*Spain: Its Greatness and Decay*. Cambridge: Cambridge UP, 1898.

Kennedy, Ruth Lee. *Studies in Tirso*. Vol. I. Chapel Hill, N. C.: U of North Carolina P, 1974.

Kern, Fritz. *Kingship and Law in the Middle Ages*. Trans. S.B. Chrimes. Oxford: Basil Blackwell & Mott Ltd., 1956.

King, Willard. "Alarcón's *Ganar amigos*: The King, the Privado, and the Law" in *Texto y Espectáculo*—Selected Proceedings of the Symposium on Spanish Golden Age Theater. 11–13 March, 1987. New York: UP of America, 1989.

___."La ascendencia paterna de Juan Ruiz de Alarcón y Mendoza." *Nueva Revista de Filología Hispánica*, 19 (1970), 49–86.

____.*Juan Ruiz de Alarcón—letrado y dramaturgo.* Mexico: El Colegio de México, 1989.

Lauer, A. Robert. *Tyrannicide and Drama.* Stuttgart: Franz Steiner Verlag, 1987.

____."The Use and Abuse of History in the Spanish Theater of the Golden Age: The Regicide of Sancho II as treated by Juan de la Cueva, Guillén de Castro, and Lope de Vega." *Hispanic Review,* 56 (1988), 17–37.

Lewy, Guenter. *Constitutionalism and Statecraft during the Golden Age of Spain: A Study of the Political Philosophy of Juan de Mariana, S.J.* Geneva: Librairie E. Droz, 1960.

Lindenberger, Herbert. *The Relation of Literature and Reality.* Chicago: U of Chicago P, 1975.

Malvezzi, Virgilio. *Historia de los primeros años del reinado de Felipe IV,* Ed. D.L. Shaw. London: Tamesis Books, Ltd.,1968.

Marañón, Gregorio. *El Conde-Duque de Olivares.* Buenos Aires: Espasa-Calpe, S.A.,1939.

Maravall, José Antonio. *Teatro y literatura en la sociedad barroca.* Madrid: Seminarios y Ediciones, S.A., 1972.

____.*La teoría del estado en el siglo XVII.* Madrid: Instituto de Estudios Políticos, 1944.

Mariana, Juan de. *Del Rey y de la Institución Real.* Biblioteca de Autores Españoles, 31 Vol. 2. Madrid: Rivadeneyra, 1854. 463–575.

Metford, J.C.J. "Tirso de Molina and the Count-Duke de Olivares." *Bulletin of Hispanic Studies* 36 (1959), 15–27.

Morley, S. Griswold, and Courtney Bruerton. *Cronología de las comedias de Lope de Vega.* Madrid: Editorial Gredos, S.A., 1968.

Pérez de Herrera, Cristóbal. *Amparo de Pobres,* Ed. Michel Cavillac. Madrid: Espasa-Calpe, S.A., 1975.

____.*Proverbios Morales,* Madrid: Luis Sánchez, 1618.

Plutarch, *Lives.* Vol. 1, 99–148, Vol. 7, 140–18, and Vol. 8, 220–222. Trans. with critical and historical notes by John Langhorne and William Langhorne, correction and additions by Rev. Frances Wrangham. Philadelphia: Brannan and Morford, 1811.

Poesse, Walter. *Juan Ruiz de Alarcón.* New York: Twayne Publishers, Inc., 1972.

Quevedo, Francisco de. *Teatro inédito de Don Francisco de Quevedo y Villegas.* "Introducción" Miguel Artigas. Madrid: Tipografía de la "Revista de Archivos," 1927.

Ruiz de Alarcón, Juan. *Obras Completas* 3 vols. Ed. Agustín Millares Carlo. Mexico: Fondo de Cultura Económica, 1957, 1959, 1968.

Somers, Melvina. "Quevedo's Ideology in *Cómo ha de ser el privado.*" *Hispania*, 39 (1956), 261–268.

Tierno Galván, Enrique. "Introducción" to *Antología de escritores políticos del Siglo de Oro.* Ed. Pedro de Vega. Madrid: Taurus, 1965.

Tirso de Molina. *Obras dramáticas completas* Vol. 3 Ed. Blanca de los Ríos. Madrid: Aguilar, 1958. 3 vols. 904–951, 1075–1116.

Tomás y Valiente, Francisco. *Los validos en la monarquía española.* Madrid, 1963; rpt. Valencia: Siglo Veintiuno Editores, 1982.

Vega Carpio, Lope Félix de. *El villano en su rincón.* In *Fuenteovejuna /El villano en su rincón.* Ed. J. Alcina Franch. Barcelona: Editorial Juventud, S.A., 1974, 169–295.

Vives, Juan Luis. *Obras—Del socorro de los pobres.* Vol. 1. Trans. Lorenzo Riber. Madrid: Aguilar, 1947.

INDEX

A

absolutism. *See also* law; obedience
  in Bodin, 1-6, 8, 10
  in Lope de Vega's plays, 43
  of Hapsburgs, 10
  and power of *privado*, 16-17
  senate for moderating, 84
agriculture. *See also* farming
  declines in, 23-24
  proposals for encouraging, 28
  in theater, 40-41
Albert, Archduke, 25
alcabalas, 28
Alfonso I, 121
Alfonso III, 126
Alfonso V, 111
ambition. *See also* honor
  marriage for advancing, 122
  of *privado*, 15-16, 114, 118
  renounced by *privado*, 67, 112-113, 131-132
  wealth required for, 81
amistad castigada, La, 74, 92-103, 110, 117, 120, 139-142, 144
Amparo de pobres, on honorable poor, 29, 30, 138
anagrams, for disguising characters, 62
Andalusia, 68
animal life, monarchy examples in, 3
annuities, proposal for, 28
Aquinas, Thomas, on rights of resistance, 8-9
Arabs, 40
Aragón, 52, 68
árbol venturoso, 86
Aristotle, 42, 44
arts
  banned by Lycurgus, 84
  king's training in, 20
  Olivares's attraction for, 67
assassination. *See* murder
audiences of king, 49
austerity, championed by Olivares, 19

of king to God, 2
of king to law, 8-9, 101-103
of *privado*, 55-56, 63
of subject to king, 2, 74

E
economic decline. *See also* Castile; reform
    chivalric mentality encouraging, 30
    and currency collapse, 25-26, 29, 43, 46
    and deficit financing, 26
    in literature, 42
    Olivares's efforts against, 67
    theater disguising, 39, 41-42
    under Philip II, 23-24
edicts. *See also* law
    for court expenses, 28, 29, 33-34, 81
    sanctity of, 88, 110, 141
education. *See also* didactic purpose
    historical knowledge for, 138
    Lycurgus's concept of, 84-85
    reform for, 1
    restricted for farmers, 29, 125
el Sabio, Alfonso, 45
England. *See also* Europe
    alliances with Spain, 64
    theater in, 39, 138
    war with Spain, 24
    wool imports from, 34
envy. *See also* gifts; honor
    criticized by Alarcón, 108
    in Tirso de Molina's plays, 53
    gifts producing, 58-59
    of *privado*, 60
equality. *See also* justice; law
    of citizens under law, 107-108, 141, 144
escribanos, proposal for restricting, 29
estates. *See also* nobles; subjects
    for confirming kingship, 10
    for deposing tyrant, 9

Ibérica

This series of scholarly monographs focuses upon sixteenth- and seventeenth-century Hispanic Theater. *Ibérica* welcomes historical and cultural studies, as well as theoretical and critical texts that would enhance our understanding of the *Comedia* as a European phenomenon. Manuscripts may be in English, Spanish or Portuguese, with a minimum of 200 pages. Inquiries and manuscripts should be directed to the General Editor:

A. Robert Lauer
Department of Spanish and Portuguese
The University of Wisconsin-Milwaukee
Milwaukee, WI 53201